ADVANCE PRAISE

The following quotations come from the due diligence report regarding Robert T. Bethel presented to the general partners of Maryland Farms, Tennessee's largest office-park complex, which was in default to twenty-three lenders for over $100 million.

"I have known Bob all his life. Bob cleaned up several businesses that Glen Roberts and I owned twenty-five years ago. He returned all of them to profitability. He knows how to make a profit. He works well with bankers on problem loans. You will be pleased with his performance."

—JEFF DYER, CHAIRMAN, FIRST AMERICAN
NATIONAL BANK KNOXVILLE, TENNESSEE, AND
FORMER TENNESSEE BANKING COMMISSIONER

"I have known him all his life. He has worked on a number of our special asset loans and has always done a good job. I have a lot of respect for his ability. He understands real estate as well as operating businesses. If you put him in charge of this credit, you will have my vote."

—PAT HARRISON, VICE CHAIRMAN, SOVRAN
BANK, NASHVILLE, TENNESSEE

"Bob has purchased several properties from us and recently bought a large apartment complex in Birmingham, Alabama, which was in default. In six months he had it back in the black. He is currently working with a number of my distressed properties. He does what he says."

—JOHN ZOLTY, HEAD OF SOUTHEASTERN PROPERTY, AETNA REALTY INVESTMENTS, INC., HARTFORD, CONNECTICUT

"I have known Bob since the REIT crash of the 1970s when I was with Chase in New York. He has done several deals with me here in Dallas. He's sharp, understands the parts of a deal, and gets it done in short order."

—PATRICK DOOLEY, EXECUTIVE VICE PRESIDENT, TEXAS COMMERCE BANK, DALLAS, TEXAS

STRENGTHEN YOUR BUSINESS

STRENGTHEN YOUR BUSINESS

FAIL-PROOF STRATEGIES
from THE MAN WHO HAS
RESCUED 77 BUSINESSES

ROBERT THOMAS BETHEL

LIONCREST
PUBLISHING

STRENGTHEN YOUR BUSINESS

Fail-Proof Strategies from the Man Who Has Rescued 77 Businesses

ISBN   978-1-61961-673-8 *Hardcover*

978-1-61961-623-3 *Paperback*

978-1-61961-622-6 *Ebook*

To my business partner, friend, and wife, Reese,
who encouraged me to write this book.

CONTENTS

FOREWORD

BY T. BOONE PICKENS

I met Bob Bethel in 1976, while we were both working in the North Sea off the coast of Scotland. It was a chance meeting, considering we shared no business connections at the time. In 1987, Bob invited me to speak at Vanderbilt's Owen Graduate School of Management and Cumberland University, where my father graduated from Law School—invitations I was happy to accept.

The next invitation I received from Bob was to write the foreword for his book, *Strengthen Your Business*, and again, I accepted.

In this book, Bob sheds light on the important lessons I've learned during my six decades in the oil industry. First is a focus on the team. I never could have built Mesa Petroleum and BP Capital into billion-dollar businesses without my team. As Bob wisely points out, getting your team involved is the first step in building a strong business regardless of your industry.

Bob also prioritizes establishing a profit mindset within your company. I believe, as Bob does, the main reason half of all businesses fail is because profit isn't emphasized from the outset. Not only does Bob reiterate this point throughout the book, he also provides a system that can be easily implemented within any business to track profits daily.

An entire chapter of *Strengthen Your Business* is devoted to the qualities of effective business leaders. I applaud Bob for instructing business owners on ways to elevate their performance and encouraging them to give their best effort.

Every country in the world depends on the kind of small and medium-sized businesses Bob aims to help with *Strengthen Your Business*. I would advise any business owner, whether times are troubled or prosperous, to study and apply the lessons Bob demonstrates. Doing so has the power to transform your business into a more efficient and profitable operation.

Boone Pickens

T. BOONE PICKENS

INTRODUCTION

WHY I'LL NEVER BE HANDSOME, SMART, RICH, OR BULLETPROOF AGAIN

There's an old joke about the four stages of drunkenness:

STAGE 1: Handsome: *"I am without a doubt the best-looking man in this bar tonight."*

STAGE 2: Smart: *"I've got it all figured out—there's no problem I can't solve."*

STAGE 3: Rich: *"I'm itching to show off how much money I've got."*

STAGE 4: Bulletproof: *"I'm untouchable. Nothing can stop me."*

After fifty-two years in business, I like to add a fifth stage for drunk businessmen:

STAGE 5: Radiation proof: *"Everything I touch turns to gold. My company will never fail."*

I've spent my career turning around seventy-seven businesses on the brink of failure. During that time, I've gotten familiar with business owners who thought they were handsome, smart, rich, bulletproof, *and* radiation proof. The more success they enjoyed, the more these obnoxious qualities were amplified. Their egos tricked them into thinking nothing bad could happen to them or their business. I'm surprised some of them didn't float away with such swollen heads.

Imagine how quickly they sobered up when I came in and bought their business for $1, because the bank was days away from seizing every asset they owned—cars, house, jewelry, and other assets—to recoup money on a loan they could no longer pay.

I can relate to the ego trip you experience when your business is successful. I've spent five decades rescuing every single business I've taken over, but I didn't start out knowing the answers I'm going to share in this book. In fact, I was once more like the drunken businessman than I care to admit.

Early in my career, I fancied myself far more handsome, rich, smart, bulletproof, and radiation proof than I was.

I'll never see myself that way again.

BY MY BOOTSTRAPS

My parents came of age during the Great Depression, and those hard times gave them a powerful work ethic they passed down to my siblings and me. I was the oldest of four, and by the age of five, I started a paper route in Nashville, Tenn. At seven, I mowed lawns, and by the time I was ten, I worked the wash rack for minimum wage at Hippodrome Ford in Nashville, Tennessee, where my dad worked as the sales manager.

By fourteen, my dad had me on the junk lot selling old used cars. The job taught me serious life lessons about both business and people that no classroom could have. I was hungry to know all I could about the dealership, everything from customer service to parts and accounting, and I soaked it all in.

I attended the University of Tennessee and studied business, but I continued selling cars all through college earning $30,000 a year. At that time, the average median household income was about $6,000.

When I finished college, I'd saved enough money to buy an underperforming auto dealership in a small town. The old man who'd owned the place sold a few cars a month, but within one year, we became one of the top ten dealerships in the four-state area.

Everything was rosy, and just like the drunk businessman I described earlier, I felt more handsome, smart, rich, bulletproof, and radiation proof with each passing year. Little did I know, however, a nationwide recession was coming.

As a rural dealership, we had to sign recourse on any sales contract we wrote up. If a customer bought a car and couldn't make his payments, we were on the hook for whatever money he still owed the bank on his loan.

The recession hit in 1971. Within weeks, cars came back to the dealership. I fought like hell to make the payments and stay afloat, but after eighteen months, I was up to my neck in debt. I could see the end of the road long before we went off the cliff. I was simply too inexperienced to know what to do.

FROM TOP OF THE WORLD TO ROCK BOTTOM

You know that old saying, "If it seems too good to be true, it probably is?" If I had heeded that warning early on, I'd have saved myself a great deal of pain.

Here's how it all went down:

Before the recession, the dealership was making money and I started a sideline in the cattle business. I bought a herd of cattle, and before my check went bad, I partnered with a banker friend of the family who backed me up. After the cattle fattened up, I sold them at a nice profit and the banker was impressed. He offered me a 50/50 partnership with loans under the table.

When a bank president says he wants to be your silent partner, you don't ask questions—you nod your head and count your lucky stars, especially when you're twenty-one years old. At least, that's how I felt. I was too high on success to realize this savvy businessman was making money off me with zero risk to himself. He was playing me like a fiddle.

Our arrangement lasted until my banker partner died unexpectedly and left me with tons of loans in my name at the bank. The banker's death coincided with the '71 recession, and I was saddled with writing checks for both cars *and* the bank loans. Failure stared me down on two fronts.

I'd awake in the middle of the night so rigid with fear I'd throw up my dinner. When I say I understand the gut-wrenching anxiety and terror that cripples the owners of failing businesses, I've got the scars to prove it. If your business is underwater or underperforming, I've been in your shoes. I'm here to help you turn things around before you hit rock bottom.

I lived at rock bottom for months, before deciding I couldn't fight anymore. I picked up the phone, called the bank, and told them I was broke, which was a huge mistake. Had I known then what I know now, I could have turned things around for myself. However, I was young, naive, and desperate for a way to stop the bleeding.

What came next was the most humiliating experience of my life. I sold my house, my antique cars, and a family farm that had been granted to my father's family after the Revolutionary War. I moved into a rental house with my wife and two young daughters, as I worked out payment plans for all the money I owed. I never declared bankruptcy, everyone got their money, and I learned how dangerous overconfidence can be when you're having success in business.

GETTING OUT FROM UNDER

I was in the depths, but luck was on my side. It turned out a man who was a good friend of my parents, and one of the wealthiest men in middle Tennessee, had been keeping an eye on my business escapades. He got a hold of me and told me point blank, "I think you've learned a valuable lesson. Now, are you ready to stop being scared and start doing something with what you have learned?"

His offer was straightforward: He had some businesses in poor shape and he wanted me to take them over, clean them up, and make them profitable. I accepted the opportunity, and I've never looked back. Turning around failing businesses became my life's work and my greatest professional passion.

GOING HOLISTIC

I benefited enormously from my weekly meetings at his house in Nashville. At our first meeting, I brought notebooks filled with financial data. "Put all that stuff away," he told me. "You and I are going to talk about our businesses and the people you have running them. The CPA can send me the financial information."

We worked that way as a team for five years, talking about business from a holistic perspective, not just from data and numbers. Those discussions reinforced the importance of learning every aspect of our businesses, not just those elements that interested me the most.

Every business we worked on either returned to profitability or maximized profit within one year. I soon found myself back in the good graces of the banking community. That's when the calls started rolling in and doors opened for me to take over more and more failing businesses.

THE LESSONS I'VE LEARNED

I've spent fifty-two years turning around businesses in every industry imaginable—automobile, restaurant, manufacturing, engineering, real estate, agriculture, marketing, retail, veterinary, multinational firms, and many more. Regardless of the industry, I ended up applying the same basic principles.

I didn't use rocket science to save seventy-seven businesses (some of which owned multiple companies, making the number closer to one hundred), more than 10,000 jobs, and the livelihoods of countless vendors who depended on those businesses for work. I used simple "meat and potatoes" strategies any business owner can plug into their company.

Better yet, I NEVER brought in new money or new people when taking over a failing operation. The businesses I stepped into had everything they needed to turn things around. All it took to get them on track were the solid business principles we'll cover in this book.

Statistics tell us 50% of all businesses fail, so if you're doing well right now, remember your long-term success is basically a coin flip. Don't be like the drunk businessman and let bullheadedness offset the courage it took to start or buy your business. The policies, procedures, and systems in this book can be failure insurance for your business if you'll try them. I've seen them work in a wide variety of industries, so I'm confident they'll work for you, too. Throughout this book, I'll use the term "turnaround," and if your business is underperforming, a turnaround begins with your thinking and the way you do business. Everything starts with your mental approach to making positive change in your business.

If you're reading this and you have dreams of starting a business, I hope to show you a blueprint for what works, and help you understand whether you're truly ready to start a business. Even the most prepared entrepreneurs are confronted with challenges they never expected.

The companies I've worked with weren't started by stupid people; they were started by people who thought business ownership would be simple. This mindset leads to mistakes, and those are what I come in and help fix with the foolproof strategy I'm going to teach you in these pages.

I'm not going to ask you to buy a fancy computer program

or hire an accountant to put everything together. Your only expense will be a few big whiteboards. The real cost of turning around a failing business is discipline and carrying out these strategies daily.

Dwell for a moment on this quote from Henry Ford: "Whether you think you can, or you think you can't— you're right."

Business owners need a healthy balance of pride and humility. You have to be confident without being arrogant. You must be wise without being a know-it-all. You should possess a healthy fear of failure without letting it consume you.

Knowing I didn't *have* to fail early in my career keeps a fire lit inside my belly, yet the fear of failure still motivates me. In large part, I've been successful seventy-seven times because one failure would have broken me financially. I couldn't afford to fail.

Now, I want to help others avoid the disastrous fallout of failing in business. We know 50% of all businesses fail. Success is a coin flip. With your help, we can influence that coin flip to turn out in your favor. You must work hard, smart, and know what to look for in your business. I'll show you the way, starting with a lesson vital to what we're doing, as you'll see in Chapter One.

DON'T COMPLICATE
MATTERS

Early in my career, Vanderbilt University started an executive MBA program. I had dealt with a lot of MBAs in my line of work, and I wondered what secrets to success these MBA programs revealed to their students. I was curious to know the truth, so I applied to Vanderbilt's new program and was accepted.

Dean Richmond of the business school only hired professors for the MBA program who had been in the private sector for years, which meant we learned practical strategies we could apply in our businesses for immediate improvement.

Working with the owners of failing businesses, I've

learned having an MBA doesn't make you immune to failure. Some programs don't prioritize practical lessons, choosing instead to focus on theories, philosophies, and financial ratios.

I want this book to benefit you in the way those classes benefited me. Theories and ratios are nice, but like any professional, I believe business owners learn the most when they ditch the textbook and talk about concrete business principles from decades of life experience. When my business partner and I would meet, we took a tactical approach to making our businesses profitable. We didn't discuss theories.

In other words, we didn't complicate matters. We didn't even discuss numbers. Oftentimes, a business owner is compelled to introduce unnecessary complexity into his business. A simpler approach might seem obvious, but that owner wants to validate his own intelligence. I've learned in my career a person's greatest strength is often their greatest weakness. These owners often shoot themselves in the foot. They're so smart, they've out-smarted themselves.

Business is not complicated unless you make it compli-cated. The principles in this book can untangle any kind of mess you've created in your business. However, you must be willing to swallow your pride and plug these strategies into problem areas so they can do their work.

I'm thankful for the applicable lessons I learned at Vanderbilt, because my livelihood depends on rapidly producing profit in businesses sometimes hemorrhaging money. The bankers I work with aren't the most patient people in the world, which means I don't have time to learn something if it doesn't advance the businesses forward.

If your business is failing or underperforming, time is a commodity you can't afford to waste. I respect that and promise to deliver actionable strategies you can immediately use to improve your business and do so quickly.

In addition to sharing my experiences, you also get to learn from my failures. If there's a mistake that can be made in business, I've made it during my career. I want to keep you from making those same mistakes. It's true getting knocked down and choosing to get back up makes you stronger. However, not having to get knocked down is pretty damn nice, too!

WHAT HAPPENS WHEN A BUSINESS BEGINS TO FAIL

To better understand the world I operate in, let me paint you a picture:

You buy an apartment complex. For the first two years, you make your payments to the bank on time and everyone is happy. Suddenly, a recession hits—vacancies go up, you lose money, and your property's appraised value is cut in half. When the crap hits the proverbial fan, the bank turns your loan over to professionals tasked with maximizing the money the bank gets back, *before* your business collapses.

These are the folks I work with—the Special Assets Department. I like to think of them as the SEAL Team Six of the banking world, because they're ruthless and they waste no time. If they don't see an immediate change in the financial situation of a company, they pull the plug. If you call a bank and ask for this department, you'll most likely be told they don't exist. I've worked with these cutthroat professionals long enough to attest to their existence. In fact, I admire their brutal efficiency so much that I named one of our businesses Special Assets Management, LLC.

If your loan ends up in the hands of the Special Assets Department, things can get painful quickly. One of the first things they'll do is foreclose on your apartment complex. If you fight them in court, the bank will turn that foreclosure over to their lawyers, which costs them time and money.

In the meantime, they're going to seize the assets you offered as collateral when you signed the personal guarantee for your loan. Your home, cars, other assets, and profitable side income streams become property of the bank. The money they recoup from your devalued apartment complex and personal property won't cover the value of the loan, though.

If your bank has $3 million set up in their loan loss reserves, and they're going to be $2 million short on your loan, it's no problem. They simply reduce loan loss reserves to $1 million. This move has no impact on the quarterly profit and loss (P&L) report they send to their shareholders. Most of the time, shareholders won't notice if the loan loss reserves drop a couple million dollars.

However, if their loan loss reserves are depleted, because they just wrote off other loans, that $2 million is coming out of their quarterly profit, and the shareholders are going to be upset. This outcome is a lose-lose situation for all parties involved.

As the managing director at Special Assets Management, LLC, I'm brought in as a happier alternative to that sad reality. Rather than pushing you to the point of bankruptcy and spending whatever money they get from your personal assets on legal fees, the bank will call and ask if I'm interested in taking over your loan.

If I say yes, I'm responsible for that $2 million deficit and owe the bank a monthly P&L and other reports, so they can track the progress of the turnaround. If that business continues losing money, or the bank isn't satisfied, they'll call the loan, and I'm screwed. I certainly don't want to be on the hook for $2 million with the bank!

The bank has two goals they hope to accomplish by handing the loan off to me:

1. Ideally, I can help turn the business around and make it profitable.
2. If I fail, the bank has time to build its loan loss reserves back up.

I have time to look over every operation beforehand and decide if it can be saved. I don't say yes to each request I get. Some are simply too far gone to pull out of the swamp.

Let's say I agree to take over your loan. I'm going to come to you and explain your business is broke, and the bank has your house and cars as collateral. Not only that, they're going to sue you to make up the deficit. Your future wages will be garnished until that deficit is paid off. You could declare bankruptcy, but that move would destroy you for years to come. You're better off accepting the deal I propose:

"If you sign over your business to me, I'll negotiate with the bank to walk away from your personal guarantee. If I can save your personal property, keep you from getting sued, and help you avoid bankruptcy, will you sell your business to me for $1?"

I've asked that question many times, and every single time, the owner said "yes" because they realize it's the smart move. The business owner gets to keep a roof over his head and a car in the driveway. The bank saves tons of time and money on legal fees.

I've taken over loans in every industry imaginable, because the core of any good business is profitability. I don't care if it's engineering or retail, if a business isn't making a profit, their glide slope with the earth is dependent on cash flow—the money the owner can borrow from banks or his relatives, or the money he has in his pockets. Regardless of how it's being kept alive, profit-starved businesses eventually go broke.

I step in when I think a turnaround is possible. Once I sign on, the problems plaguing that business become my concern. Regardless of what I find when I roll up my sleeves and get to work, it's my butt on the line now. Failure is no longer an option.

To be honest, even after fifty-two years, I never know what I'm walking into on day one.

WHAT A FAILING BUSINESS LOOKS LIKE

One company I took over was a large manufacturing facility. The company was seven years old, had over one hundred employees, and produced about fifteen products. It was also $6 million in debt. The two men who owned it had never made a profit.

When I walked into the facility for the first time, it was like you could smell failure in the air. Every employee I walked past looked scared and beaten down. Their demeanors reflected the tension and anxiety that permeates most failing businesses. The few I talked to had a general sense the business was struggling, but none of them knew just how bad things had gotten.

Welding was the primary focus of this manufacturing facility. I signed on, because I had owned a world-class engineering company. My company had once produced 3,000 miles of weld without a defect while working on the manufacturing of nuclear reactors and nuclear steam generators for the nuclear division of Westinghouse Electric. Coming into this company, I knew what proper welding looked like. We worked for Westinghouse for seven years and quickly learned perfection is required in the nuclear industry.

The minute I stepped foot in the welding shop, I knew none of the welders had been properly trained. Their collective performance was poor and indicated to me they'd learned on the job. Something as simple as the gas coverage of the welding process was all screwed up. Rather than setting the gas level correctly, which is essential for a good weld, every welding station had the gas wide open. I got in touch with a welding expert I'd worked with before, and he immediately trained them.

A lack of proper training is a hallmark of failing businesses. Where there should be precision, you find a disorganized mess. The welding shop was just the first example in this facility.

After visiting the welding shop, I walked into the bookkeeping office and asked to see the pricing book. When I opened the three-inch thick binder the bookkeeper handed me, my jaw nearly hit the floor. The couple hundred customers in that book each had their own price list! I took that binder straight into the office of the owner in charge of sales and asked him to explain this madness. His response blew my mind:

"Well, we all know you've got to beat your competition."

As he explained it, the company's sales strategy was to meet with business owners who were buying from our competitors, find out what they paid for the products our facility sold, and undercut the prices the competition was charging. Now I understood why every customer had their own price list. I did some back-of-the-napkin accounting as I sat there and realized they were losing money on 75% of their sales. The owner who worked offsite had no idea pricing was being handled this way.

Both owners loved to beat their chests about gross sales but were stumped as to why they kept losing money. When I explained they were essentially selling $5 bills for $4, their confusion ended, and I eliminated their wacky pricing strategy.

What I found in that facility reinforced the notion failing businesses are rarely profit-minded. The owners I purchased the facility from had no grasp of accounting or sales strategy. Their collective ignorance started the company down a path that sounded smart but pushed them toward bankruptcy. They didn't run the business off the cliff on purpose; they just didn't know any better. Most failing businesses are the same way.

The next rock I turned over in the facility revealed another staple of failure: dysfunction. At the first meeting I called, I told the staff I would now be signing off on all purchases. Yet, when I walked past the purchase manager's office an hour later, I overheard him discussing shipment of $300,000 worth of steel he'd just purchased.

It was all I could do to keep from yelling. I calmly asked him if he understood what I said in the meeting about wanting to sign off on all purchases. A red tinge crept across his face as he explained, "I thought you were talking about office supplies."

My favorite part of his explanation came when he told me he bought $300,000 worth of steel instead of a smaller amount, because buying that much was easier for the tow motor drivers to unload. If I hadn't been so angry, I'd have laughed. God bless him, the man's heart was in the right place. His brain? Not so much.

I'd taken over a broke company, whose employees spent $300,000 without approval on more steel than we needed for the next three weeks, yet couldn't buy purchase order books without approval from the owner's wife who managed office supplies. I don't say this to make fun of anybody, but rather to show you why businesses suffer. When owners are out of touch with reality, employees are kept in the dark, and the entire operation is riddled with inefficiencies and dysfunction—the business is headed for disaster.

AREA OF FOCUS #1 FOR HEALTHY BUSINESSES: KNOWING WHERE YOU STAND

My first area of focus in a new company is implementing a system that tells every employee where we stand at any given moment. In failing businesses, this information is obscured from employees, which breeds an atmosphere of miscommunication and distrust. Thriving businesses rally around a shared purpose and celebrate transparency, and turnarounds are only possible when all employees become fully committed to what you're trying to accomplish.

One way to earn their buy-in is to institute a system that allows everyone to know where the business stands always. In Chapter Four, I'll show you how to implement that system with "headlight accounting," but for now, understand that transparency and a shared purpose is where it all begins.

If I take over a business and can't tell the bank how we're doing at a given moment, the Special Assets Department is going to eat my lunch. I value knowledge of my financial standing the way I value oxygen, and you should, too. If you don't, you could be paddling downstream thinking everything's fine while your boat is taking on water.

I once worked with two veterinarians whose business got in trouble for reasons unbeknownst to them. These were two of the most well-respected equine vets in Tennessee who appeared to be doing everything right on the surface of their business, yet they were still suffering. One day, after working on my horses, they asked if I'd look at their practice, and I happily agreed.

The first question I asked when I visited their office was how they priced their services. One of the vets told me every six months their secretary called and quoted the other vet offices for services like a rabies vaccination. Once they had everyone's prices, they simply offered their rabies vaccine cheaper than anyone else. To them, this seemed like a savvy business tactic.

To me, it sounded like the gooney bird theory of pricing. Have you heard of the gooney bird? It flies in smaller and smaller concentric circles, until it flies up its own ass.

We'd found money pit number one. My next question was on the inventory of drugs they kept at the office. They proudly told me they ordered drugs from a veterinary pharmaceutical firm in Memphis, and if their order was placed before 4 pm, they'd get the drugs the following morning by 10 am. They were very proud of not carrying an inventory. If the drug they ordered cost $10, they doubled the price and charged people $20 for it.

When I looked through their books, even after doubling the price, they weren't covering the cost of shipping those drugs through FedEx. Every time they treated an animal with drugs, they were losing money. Here was money pit number two.

Another look at their books showed me where 90% of their income was originating: truck driving. Because their services were so cheap, and they were losing money on the drugs, their main source of income was charging mileage plus a fee for driving two huge equine trucks housing tons of expensive equipment.

Once we raised their pricing to an appropriate level and changed their terms of payment from 30 days to one week, their cash flow improved, and they made the kind of money they should've made all along.

The two owners of this practice graduated from Texas A&M and were both brilliant doctors, but like they told me when we examined their issues together, they never had classes about running a business. Like most business owners, they'd gravitated toward their field of interest, started a business, and dealt with any challenges as best they could. They ran into trouble the same way a lot of business owners do: They didn't know what they didn't know.

Knowing what we know about business failure rates, and the crash course business owners receive on the job, it's imperative you know how your business is doing always. You can't rely on monthly reports that show a snapshot of the previous month. What if cash flow dries up January 1 and you don't find out until forty days later? What if your accountant repeats a costly mistake thirty times, before you catch it?

Taillight accounting—looking back at your business over the past month—doesn't help you succeed moving forward, so in Chapter Four, we'll turn on your headlights.

AREA OF FOCUS #2 FOR HEALTHY BUSINESSES: TOP-DOWN PROBLEM-SOLVING

Once you know the status of your business at any given moment, the second area of focus is solving problems from the top down. When I come into a new business, I know a good deal about what's going, but I'm not arrogant enough to think I have it all figured out. To solve the problems plaguing the operation, I leverage the greatest asset any business owner has—the TEAM. We'll cover this topic in depth in Chapter Two, but the team is always my go-to problem-solving resource.

In addition to a company-wide meeting I convene on the first day, I meet individually with every employee and ask for their unfiltered feedback. They open up to me, because I promise them nothing they say will come back to bite them in the butt.

I always left those meetings knowing exactly what was wrong in the company based on what the employees told me. Their insights were invaluable.

The banks always ask me why the previous owner didn't utilize the collective knowledge of his team. The answer has always been obvious to me. Why on earth would an employee working for a bullheaded owner put their future on the line by telling that owner something he didn't want to hear? Employees are smart enough to know the answer their boss wants to hear, and often it's not the truth.

To continue paying their mortgage and putting food on the table, the employees wisely choose to tell the owner what he wants to hear, knowing full well even if they offered up meaningful suggestions, the owner would simply continue running things how he wanted.

I continue to use "he" and "his," because every business I've taken over was run by a man. A large part of the reason male-driven businesses get in trouble is because of ego. The drunken businessman views himself as smarter, richer, and better looking than everyone. Is he going to listen to his employees? Will he even seek their input?

I've learned hiring women for high-level positions is extremely healthy for companies. Women aren't hampered by ego like men and tend to use common sense more. When it comes to the financials, I've watched men round up to the nearest hundred dollars all my life. A woman in that position will stay at the office all night balancing her books down to the last penny. Women value precision, which is a sterling trait for CEOs or presidents of businesses to have during a turnaround.

Regardless of gender, a top-down approach to problem-solving works best when business owners see themselves as the conductor of an orchestra. If one member of an orchestra is playing the wrong note, the collective performance suffers. I meet with every employee in a new business, from the managers down to the janitors, because each of them and their families is invested in the success of that company.

As the conductor, I'm always asking my team, "How can we do things faster, cheaper, smarter, and better?" I want every employee to play their part during the process of change we're undergoing.

People ask me what I do for a living, and the best words I've found to use are "teacher" and "coach." In each of my businesses, it's my job to teach and coach the team to think, not just act. I can recall countless times well-intentioned employees did a bad job, because they didn't stop to think. A prime example was the head of maintenance for a real estate development, who made $20 an hour, marching into my office and proudly telling me he and two other guys, each making $15 an hour, had fixed the commercial vacuum cleaner.

The maintenance crew had worked earnestly to do a good job. The only problem was the vacuum cost $200 to replace, and their collective labor cost $400. As a business owner, teaching your team is a huge priority because it's an ongoing process of growth. It's not enough to get them involved in the turnaround of the company. When you learn something new, teach it to your team. The more time and effort you invest in educating your employees, the stronger your company will be.

Being a business owner also means being a leader. As

I've studied history, I don't recall Winston Churchill or Franklin D. Roosevelt being called managers, although they were. They are always referred to as leaders. Being a leader is not always easy. I crashed and burned in my first business in large part due to my young age and not being experienced enough to run a business, but I was also too concerned about the employees liking me. Now, I don't care if employees like me; I'm more interested in their performance as team members.

I'm going to treat the team fairly, be honest with them, and act consistently from one day to the next. If I expect my employees to show up at 7 am and leave at 5 pm, I'll be there at 6:30 am and leave at 5:30 pm. What I expect in return are employees who want to be team players and contribute to our company's journey and profitability.

You'll be amazed at how effective and honest leadership improves the performance of your business. I always try to keep the CEO around when I take over a new business, because he's a good source of insight. However, like my dad said, "Put me in a room full of horse crap, and I'll start looking for the pony." In all seventy-seven businesses, part of the solution was firing the CEO, because his ineffective leadership was sabotaging our progress.

As the owner, the turnaround of your company starts with

you, but you can't implement top-down problem-solving unless you get everyone involved. Teach your team and value their ideas. You'll still make the ultimate decision, but I promise you some of the best ideas for aiding your turnaround will come from the places you least expect.

AREA OF FOCUS #3 FOR HEALTHY BUSINESSES: PRIORITIZE PROFITABILITY

Early in the process of starting a business, you're going to have a lot of meetings—with lawyers to legally start the business, with a Realtor to look at facilities, with a drafts person to draw out ideas, and with someone to handle payroll. Once the business is off the ground, you'll meet with your team to discuss all manner of business minutia.

Do you know what topic you likely won't talk about during those early meetings?

How to make the company profitable.

Business owners need to be told, "You've got to make a profit." You can misconstrue that statement as me demeaning the intelligence of business owners, but that's not my intent. I have deep respect for people who buy or start a business, but I think most of them start at a disadvantage, because they lack general management knowledge. The equine veterinarians I knew used the gooney bird theory of pricing, because they weren't born knowing how to run a business.

This book is a Band-Aid for that lack of knowledge, and if there's one meat and potatoes principle I stress above all others, it's this: You must prioritize PROFIT from day one.

I'm not talking about cash flow. Thirty years ago, a senior executive of Westinghouse Electric Corporation told me, "Our cash flow is so large we could be broke for eighteen months before knowing it." I imagined them like a hamster on a wheel, bringing in tons of money through the front doors without knowing if they were sinking.

Did you know Amazon only made a profit as of recently? The stock market and their massive cash flow kept them in business until that point. Small and medium-sized businesses don't have that luxury. It's vitally important everyone understands from day one profit is the focus. If that's not your focus, the money you can get from banks, relatives, and your own bank account will eventually dry up.

One of the best ways I know to increase profit is to cut expenses. At least twice a year in every business I've owned, we called a timeout to re-bid our vendors. We sat down as an entire organization, employed zero-based budgeting and carefully examined each expense to see what costs we could cut. I involved every employee, because they knew better than I did what expenses were essential and which weren't. Those meetings also taught them to thoughtfully examine their department for ways to reduce expense.

I don't focus as much on increasing revenue to make failing businesses more profitable. Here's why: When I consider taking over a business, I have a meeting with the owner to assess the situation. So many of them tell me all they need is a little more capital and to raise their sales, thereby increasing revenue and their profit. What they fail to realize is they're in trouble because they already borrowed too much money, and they did so while their operations were inefficient and ineffective.

Those businesses don't need more money on day one; they need to trim the fat.

That's why you won't see sales or marketing mentioned in this book. Would you enter a sick horse in a race or fill up your gas tank if you knew there was a hole in it?

The same logic applies to your business. Unless you are operating with a plan, are on top of expenses, and are running a "lean and mean" operation, you're wasting money by chasing additional revenue without knowing what the results will be.

Once your business is meeting the goals of your plan, you can call the team together to create a marketing plan and pursue additional revenue. Until then, you prioritize profitability by reducing expenses (we'll cover this in Chapter Four).

Profitability is the number one factor that can swing the 50/50 odds of business success in your favor and keep you from being on the ugly side of that statistic. We've discussed providing your team with a financial education, but for a culture of profitability to flourish in your company, you must educate yourself, too. You can't ignore the departments in your business that fall outside your area of expertise. Trusting your team to make wise decisions and empowering them to do so is important, but you have to know what's going on in your company across the board to be an effective leader.

I didn't know anything when I worked at the car dealership, but I opened myself up to learning, and it made me a better businessman.

An orchestra conductor can't address the violin player's

issues unless he knows what part the violin is playing, and how it should be played. You should understand the role each department plays within your company and be able to measure their success. Otherwise, how can you hope to solve the problems that will inevitably arise?

Of course, it's not enough to simply achieve profitability. Sustained profitability is the goal, but ego can make that goal much harder to achieve. Owners who get a small taste of success can transform into the drunken businessman who's smarter, richer, and more handsome than everyone else. He's bulletproof, and his business is radiation proof. In his mind, the good times are going to roll on indefinitely.

Don't let arrogance submarine your company's growth. I thought my automobile dealership was going to stay in business forever, then a recession hit, which I was unprepared to deal with, and I lost everything. Things turn on a dime in the business world. If you want to safeguard against failure, keep an open mind to the strategies we're discussing. I didn't sit down to write a book after five years and a few successful turnarounds. I've been at this for five decades and have learned through trial and error across multiple industries what works and what doesn't.

Leveraging the strengths of my team was critical to each

turnaround I oversaw. Let's jump into Chapter Two and see how exactly business owners go about doing that.

LEVERAGE YOUR GREATEST ASSET

When I was young, my dad taught me the two most important phrases in business: "you're hired" and "you're fired." As a business owner, if you do a good job with the first two words, you'll seldom have to worry about the last two. While I've had employees who fired themselves for knowingly violating company policy, I've only had to fire a handful of people during my fifty-two years of taking over dysfunctional, inefficient companies.

I don't go into a business as the new owner and slash staff. The employees who are there have valuable insight and are invested in the company's future. Coming in as an outsider, I must leverage my greatest asset—the team—to have any hope of turning the business around. I can't do my job unless the employees are doing their jobs at a high level and are completely onboard with our collective mission.

What I find in failing companies are employees who are underutilized, misinformed, and disconnected. They feel like outsiders in their own workplace, because the previous owner withheld all the financial information from them. As we discussed in Chapter One, shutting your employees out breeds a culture of miscommunication and distrust. If the people you hire are intelligent and capable, they're smart enough to know things are going poorly, especially when failure tends to hang over a company like a dark cloud.

The funny part is most employees tend to overestimate how bad things are within the company. By keeping team members in the dark and allowing them to fill in the blanks on their own, the previous owner made things worse for everyone. To paraphrase Franklin D. Roosevelt, our greatest fear is fear itself. It's the unknown employees fear the most. When you bring that information to the light, the fear subsides.

I'm not saying owners should publicize payroll information. I'm saying your people should be able to answer the question, "How's the company doing?" without resorting to a shrug and their best guess.

As we'll see, one of your responsibilities as the owner is to establish a measurement of success everyone can understand. Shutting employees out of information shuts them down and keeps them from feeling validated by their job. Bring them into the loop and there will be a fresh wave of energy and enthusiasm sweeping through the business.

Over the past five decades, I haven't turned around seventy-seven failing businesses—*WE have*. When you have the full support of your team, you can achieve anything.

OWNERS FORGET WHAT IT'S LIKE TO BE AN EMPLOYEE

If a business owner's greatest asset is his team, why do so many owners fail to utilize that asset to its greatest potential? Why do employees so often feel like outsiders in their own company? One reason is owners often misjudge the impact of bad news.

Before I take over a new company, I'll sit down for a conversation with the owner and ask him if the employees know the condition of the company. Every time I've asked that question, I've gotten some variation of the same response: "Oh God, no."

These owners mistakenly believed if their employees knew the company was struggling, they'd all be out looking for new jobs. I know that logic is flawed, because I've never had an employee quit after learning of their company's struggles.

Hunting for a new job is not fun. Nobody wants to go home and tell their family they can't pay the mortgage or put food on the table because they quit their job. Your employees' livelihood is tied into the company's future. They're invested in your success.

Business owners who isolate themselves tend to forget this fact. I've been there and can attest to the loneliness that comes with owning a business. When it's your name on the loan, and you've risked everything you own to start or buy a business, it can feel like you're carrying the weight of the world on your shoulders. However, when you place yourself on an island, you ignore the reality that every employee deals with risk.

It's true you could lose everything if the business fails, but your employees could lose everything, too. Success and failure never fall solely on the owner's shoulders. If you ask your team for help, they will rise to the challenge and shoulder that burden with you.

I've seen employees make personal sacrifices for the good of the company. When I took over a large metalworking plant nestled among the hills and valleys of eastern Tennessee, an older machine operator came up to me after our first company-wide meeting, where I told everyone the business was in trouble. He stared at the floor as he sheepishly said:

"I appreciate you telling us where we are. My kids are grown, and my wife has a good job. We've paid off our house and cars. If it helps, I can go without a paycheck for a month."

That machine operator was willing to make a personal sacrifice because he was invested in the plant's future success. He wanted to be part of the solution instead of running away at the first sign of trouble. In various industries across five decades, I can tell you his attitude is shared by the vast majority of employees who learn their company is in trouble.

When people are invested in something, they'll do whatever they can to help steer it away from failure and toward success. Here's how you begin that process in your business.

GET EVERY EMPLOYEE INVOLVED IN THE TURNAROUND

On day one as the new owner, I call a company-wide

meeting that includes everyone on the payroll. Once we're all assembled, I tell them we're going to lock the doors, take the phones off the hook, and dig into the good, the bad, and the ugly of our company. I'm completely open and honest with the team and answer any questions they have.

If you're an existing owner who's withheld financial information (like P&L reports) from your employees, you can't go from being secretive to being an open book overnight. Start by explaining to your team that you're going to do things differently and ask for their input. Ease into the process and focus on teaching. Your employees are eager to learn and do a good job. Most of the time, they're dependent on you to educate them.

We'll cover topics like accounting in this book, but if you don't feel comfortable teaching your team about accounting by the end of it, buy an hour of your accountant's time. Tell them you're planning to share P&L reports with your team, and you need to be able to explain the data in a way they can understand. Don't be ashamed by what you don't know. You're doing your company a great service by broadening your knowledge base.

I know there's fear attached to opening the books and showing employees the truth, warts and all. I was so ashamed when my dealership was failing, I couldn't even tell my wife the truth. If you open up, two amazing things will happen right away:

1. Once employees are aware of the problems, improvement happens rapidly.
2. The weight of the world will lift off your shoulders.

When you're ready to have that company-wide meeting, keep a level-headed approach. You don't need to be a cheerleader and you shouldn't be down in the dumps. I've found quiet confidence works best when you're delivering bad news.

I never look forward to the first meeting, but I know it's important. Employees tend to get that wide-eyed expression when I lay all the facts on the table. Once the shock wears off, I've found this meeting serves as a "rally the troops" moment.

Employees who take pride in their company and have a personal stake in its success don't want to sit around and wallow in self-pity. They'd rather get to work fixing the problems we need to fix. As I said, when you involve employees in a process they were previously shut out of, they'll vigorously attack whatever challenges you face.

At the end of our conversation—and this step is essential—I reiterate that the company can be saved. As an owner, it's my job to inject positivity into an inherently negative situation and turn the minds of my employees toward solutions, not problems. Once everyone understands a turnaround is possible, I add this crucial caveat:

You all are the ones who will make this turnaround happen. I need each of you to take ownership of this process and share your ideas for improving profitability.

Every time I finish that initial meeting, I have employees come up to me and say: "We all knew it was bad, but we honestly thought it was a lot worse. We can make this work."

They're exactly right—with your team behind you, a turnaround is possible.

CREATING A PLAN AND CUTTING EXPENSES

Once the employees understand their role in turning things around, I explain to them that we'll use two major tools to accomplish our goal:

1. A ninety-day plan broken down into thirty-day and weekly increments

2. Regular meetings focused on cutting expenses

At the mention of a ninety-day plan, everyone's eyes glaze over. You get the sense they're all thinking the same thing: "Aw crap, not one of those useless things."

The mood in the room improves considerably when I explain we're not creating a three-inch thick Harvard business plan. We want a mission plan that lays out who is going to do what to whom, when, and for how much for the next ninety days. We'll project expected revenue and identify expenses, essential and otherwise. Once we have those data points in hand for the next ninety days, we'll break the plan into thirty-day and weekly increments.

We'll discuss plans in depth in Chapter Three, but the guts of the turnaround are found in that first meeting. Once you educate everyone on what is expected of them and what they should expect of their coworkers, you create alignment throughout the company that makes the over-arching goal of increasing profit easier to achieve.

The next step is scheduling regular meetings focused on cutting expenses. As I mentioned last chapter, I don't go into a company expecting to increase revenue because that requires me to throw money at a problem without being able to control the outcome. I can always control our expenses and eliminate costs that aren't essential to our success, but, again, I'm not equipped to handle this task alone.

I often joke that my greatest strength in business is knowing exactly how dumb I am. I've never marched into a company and slashed the budget, because I have no idea what should be cut. I hand that process over to the team and rely on their expertise.

It doesn't matter if you're a new owner or founded the company fifty years ago—your employees know the intricacies of their department better than you. They can tell you whether a piece of equipment is used often or can be sold, or whether cheaper materials would lessen product quality too dramatically.

Your employees are the ones who should dictate which costs are essential, which can be scaled back, and which can be eliminated. Owners have other concerns on their minds and can't know the little areas of savings the way their team does.

THE SPECIFICS OF CUTTING EXPENSES

When you put the task of expense reduction to your team, don't attach a percentage to it. Let them decide on their own what percentage of your expenses are expendable. Artificial thresholds place unnecessary pressure on employees and force them to cut areas they wouldn't otherwise touch. If you let the team help steer the ship, you'll be amazed by the work they do.

The seventy-seven companies I took over were not mom-and-pop corner stores. In fact, three of the businesses had annual revenue more than $300 million. Nevertheless, the team reduced expenses by *at least* 34% in each of the companies I took over. Even more amazing is the fact I never cut a single penny myself. I laid out the goal of increased profit, explained cutting expenses was the way to get there, and got out of the way.

If you're an existing owner, however, you do have a role in reducing company expenses. While your employees examine their departments for cost-saving ideas, examine what you cost the company and commit to reducing those costs. When I take over a company, I explain to the team I won't be taking a salary, but instead will take a monthly draw against future profit, and it will just be large enough to take care of my family's needs. They are not going to bust their butts so I can have a huge salary, and I don't blame them.

I've learned owners are usually the biggest source of

unnecessary expense in a company, whether it's an expense account for entertaining, a company plane, boats, a company house in Aspen or Florida, or a private secretary for their wife.

Your employees wouldn't dare ask you to cut your perks, so you've got to do it. Be up front with the team about your efforts to lessen your financial footprint. That way, employees will perceive you as being part of the solution and not part of the problem.

Banks were always amazed when I told them expenses were cut by 34% or more. When they asked how I did it, I told them I didn't—the team did. In every business I've helped turn around, I accepted up to 5% of the credit (and that's probably being generous). The other 95% belongs to the team. They are the ones who lifted us out of our rut.

WHY YOU REALLY DO NEED EVERYONE

When dealing with company-wide issues like profit, you want to bring everyone into the meeting so they can hear the news directly from you. Avoid the temptation to bring in managers and have them disseminate the message. Here's why that's a bad idea:

First, your managers might get it wrong when relaying

the information to their team. Even if they relay it with 100% accuracy, information reliability degrades as it's passed from one person to another. Remember that game Telephone you used to play in school, where the message got jumbled up as it passed among the students? It gets played every day in the business world, except the consequences aren't nearly as funny.

For example, if you tell your managers during the first meeting the company is in for hard times the next few months, they could go back to their departments and say, "Old dumb ass said we're probably going broke." It's the same sentiment, but employees need to hear your message without anyone else's spin attached to it.

Second, you don't want employees feeling like subordinates if you're expecting them to assist with the company's turnaround. Everyone on your team is an asset, and you can express that sentiment by including all employees in your first company-wide meeting, then inviting them back for any regular meetings where you discuss expenses.

One of the reasons owners have told me they don't hold company-wide meetings is they're afraid the company's financial status could become public knowledge. It's a totally reasonable concern. One of your employees blabs to the right person and suddenly your banker is in your office saying he heard rumors the company is in trouble.

Here's what you say to your team during that first meeting to avoid this problem: "I'm going to share financial information with you all, and I'm asking it stays within the walls of this company. If it gets out, it could jeopardize our relationship with the bank, vendors, and our clients. It could crush our cash flow. We have to keep this to ourselves."

With some companies, I've had friends who were related to my employees, and I've tested whether our information was leaked. To the best of my knowledge, what we talked about never reached the streets. Expectations need to be set at the outset.

IMPROVE YOUR OPERATIONS WITH PRODUCTION MEETINGS

In addition to expense meetings, you should hold company-wide production meetings to discuss any operational hold-ups. These meetings aren't about pointing fingers. I expect my employees, as members of a cohesive team, to listen when constructive feedback is offered up regarding their department. Nobody is allowed to get defensive.

Some of the best ideas I've seen for company improvement

came from lower ranking employees. One of my favorites was from a welder in the engineering company I talked about in Chapter One. We were doing projects all over the world, but our production schedule was about to hit an eight-week lull. I didn't want to lay off any of the twenty-five members of our talented welding staff, so I asked the department manager for ideas to fill the gap.

The manager called a meeting of the welding team, in which one welder suggested we look for high-tech projects around town the team could tackle during the downtime. Once we gave the thumbs up, the welding team busted butt to find available work, and within twenty-four hours, we booked a month's worth of projects that netted us substantial profit. We turned this into a new profit center.

Sometimes all you need for a brilliant solution is a fresh set of eyes to look over a problem your company is facing. Whether that's someone who works in another department or a new employee with experience in another facility, the insight of "outsiders" should never be dismissed. Creative problem-solvers need to be encouraged to share their ideas.

In addition to being a goldmine of new ideas, production meetings keep the departments within your company running at the same speed. If manufacturing is producing

1,000 units a day, and sales can only move one hundred, that miscommunication is killing your cash flow. Once you start your employees down the path to profitability in the first meeting, issues like this will inevitably crop up. Use production meetings to get your teams back in sync.

One challenge of holding company-wide meetings is staying productive during that time. To keep things moving, install these basic meeting parameters on day one:

- Plan meetings at least one week out so everyone can mark their calendars and come prepared.
- Keep meetings shorter than thirty minutes. Anything longer will drag.
- Send out an agenda ahead of time and discuss only those topics.
- If someone brings up a valid point not covered on the agenda, tell them you'll plan another meeting soon to give their issue the attention it deserves.
- Hold stand-up meetings. It's harder to fall asleep when you're standing up!

Since time is money and attention spans are short, brief meetings work wonders. You also avoid the paranoia that accompanies a managers-only meeting when you invite everyone. You can still hold management meetings, but do so as infrequently as possible. Over the years, I have asked team members what they think about when they see a closed-door, managers-only meeting. The answer is always the same: TROUBLE. Ask yourself, how would you feel being out of the loop?

Finally, if you need to meet individually with an employee, you don't have to meet in your office with the doors closed (unless you're firing them). Stop by their area during the day and talk with the doors open. The employee will be more relaxed that way, and you can continue fostering an atmosphere of open and honest communication.

NOT EVERY EMPLOYEE WILL BE A BELIEVER

One of the stumbling blocks I had to overcome in new businesses was employee doubt. With the old owner gone and the business clearly in trouble, employees had every right to be skeptical of an outsider trying to fix things with such a simple approach.

I've painted a rosy picture of employee enthusiasm and involvement so far, because that's been my experience most of the time. With that said, it's naive to think every employee will be onboard with your turnaround efforts. Whether you're coming in fresh or working in your own business, you will always deal with skeptics.

Here's how I handled one such doubter years ago: During our one-on-one meetings, the head of an important department within the company was clearly unimpressed with me and my ideas. His arms were crossed, his posture was defensive, and all the answers he gave were one or two words. After a few minutes, I was getting steamed.

Finally, I snapped at him, "Let me ask you this, based on what you've heard so far, what do you think our chances of success are?"

He replied, "I don't think you can do it, but I'm going to sit back and see."

I was more hotheaded in my younger years and his comment flew all over me. I jumped out of my seat and fired back, "No, you're not! I'll be damned if I'm going to pay someone to sit back and watch. You go pick your check up, I don't need you anymore."

Suddenly, this big, tough guy turned totally white.

"Wait a minute, wait a minute," he stammered.

"No, we're done here," I told him. "It's been obvious since the minute I walked into this company you're not a team player, you're going to stick your foot out and trip us up, because you don't think we can do it. We don't need anyone like that here."

"Give me another chance," he asked. I think in his mind he could see his salary going up in smoke and having to search for a new job.

As angry as I was, I didn't want to fire the guy. He oversaw a large department that had to operate efficiently for us to have any hope of turning things around. So, when he asked me for another chance, I was glad to give it to him.

Over the next seven years he worked at the company, this manager was a changed man. He spoke up at meetings and brought innovative ideas to the table. Despite his initial disinterest, he became one of our company's strongest leaders.

A year after that first meeting, I took him out for a beer and asked him, "Do you still think we can't do it?" We both died laughing and became good business friends.

When you're bringing employees into the fold and holding regular meetings to improve productivity and efficiency, you might have some doubters who need further convincing. Don't overreact to their skepticism and almost fire them like I did.

Instead, listen to their concerns, be honest in your response, and re-emphasize expectations. Approach the issue with a caring mindset, and you'll avoid making the mistake I did.

MAKE TEACHING AND LEARNING A HIGH PRIORITY

One of the most important duties of a business owner is to set expectations. When I take over a new company, I make it clear I'll be teaching and coaching the team what I know about the financial side of business—cash flow, cash reserves, profitability, etc. If you placed a P&L report or a balance sheet in front of your employees tomorrow, could they interpret the information in those documents? In my experience, certain costs like utilities and payroll jump out to them, but otherwise, it's like I'm asking them to read Chinese.

Employees hold the key to reducing expenses, but you as the owner must teach them what a successful company looks like. That's why when people ask me what I do for a living, I tell them I teach and coach others about profitability. As we discussed earlier, if you're not confident enough in your financial knowledge to teach, educate yourself and share what you learn with your team. However, don't delay—if profitability improves and employees demand raises, it's too late to teach them about cash reserves. It's your job in the first meeting to point out that in order to prepare for the long term, the company must reduce debt as well as build a strong cash reserve.

If you think veteran employees who've put in fifteen years or more with the same company don't want to learn, you're dead wrong. I've taken over companies full of tough old guys and gals with eighth grade educations. Looking at them, it's the last group you'd expect would want to learn about accounting. Time and again, I've watched as these folks took notes, asked intelligent questions, and showed real excitement as they learned. Afterwards, they thanked me, because they felt better equipped to do their jobs.

Your employees are hungry for knowledge, so make it clear in your company that teaching is a priority and everyone is expected to learn and grow together.

TENSION AND CONFLICT SHOULD NOT BE TOLERATED

I once took over a company with about 150 employees, ten departments, and a horrible company culture. I could feel the tension in the air the minute I walked through the doors. Everybody was griping at each other and pointing fingers at other departments.

The first thing I did was schedule company-wide lunch

meetings for the next ten weeks. Each week, one department educated the rest of us on what they did within the company, and every member of that department participated in the presentation.

Within three weeks, the atmosphere in the company had completely changed. The bickering had ceased, and employees from different departments who had never interacted talked regularly. Those presentations broke down the walls that kept our team from feeling unified and cleared up the misconceptions hindering our communication. It made such a difference I made lunch presentations a fixture of my future turnarounds.

A healthy company culture is vital, not only for a turnaround, but also for sustained profitability, and one of the quickest ways to poison that culture is with internal conflict. I make it known in the first company-wide meeting that conflict will not be tolerated. I leave room for debate and disagreement, but demand our conversations always be civil and respectful. If employees can't meet this expectation, as I like to say, they fire themselves.

If your business is struggling or not achieving the profit it should, I can guarantee your issues are internal. I've sat with seventy-seven business owners who all told me their problems were external—banks wouldn't extend loans, customers didn't pay on time, the economy was in the tank, etc. Every time, the problems that kept the company from being profitable came from within.

I know the issues that cross your desk as the owner can run you ragged. I liken it to the story of the two crows perched next to the airport watching a Learjet do touch-and-goes. One crow turned to the other and said, "Boy, that bird's fast!" The other said, "If you had two assholes and both were on fire, you'd be fast, too!"

When you're the boss, it can feel like you're moving a million miles an hour and not getting anywhere some days. One thing you do not have time for is babysitting upset employees. Make it clear to your team you're not going to pay good money for them to be at odds with their coworkers. Issues must be dealt with in a rational manner.

While I don't consider it my responsibility to babysit, part of my job as the owner is to keep my ear to the ground and know when conflict is brewing. If I have two department heads who are at odds, I'm going to sit them down and ask them to work out whatever logistical issue is creating tension. Being proactive keeps the conflict from escalating and hurting the company. As an owner and a leader, that is part of your job description.

PERFORMANCE REVIEWS HELP EMPLOYEES THRIVE

I've never understood why performance reviews elicit such a negative reaction. Over the years, I've watched employees sit in my office so nervous they sweat profusely and stumble over their words. You'd think I'd called them in for a root canal!

We become accustomed to being graded from the time we're very young. Depending on the level of education, some teams have upwards of twenty years of experience being evaluated in school every six or eight weeks. So, why isn't everyone regularly evaluated in the workforce? Shouldn't business owners be as concerned with the performance of employees—which impacts profitability and livelihoods—as schools and parents are about student performance?

Performance evaluations let employees know where their strengths are and where they need to improve. It's also an opportunity to specifically recognize outstanding work. Don't be like the owner I watched walk through his manufacturing plant, patting everyone on the back and telling all of them they were doing a great job. Not only is that feedback vague and meaningless, it pisses off your employees who are actually doing good work to have their effort compared to that of coworkers they know are slacking off.

When I hold performance reviews, I open the discussion by asking employees for areas they feel they could improve. I do this, so they won't be defensive or feel like they're being attacked. Instead, the employees are now engaged in a thoughtful discussion about helping them improve. I want everyone on my team to understand I'm there to help them, not chew their butt for any deficiencies I see in their performance.

One way we help employees is by paying for any classes they want to take. It doesn't matter if the class is online, taught at a university, or hosted at the local YMCA. The class doesn't even have to pertain to their job. No matter the subject or the setting, the company will pay for the class. I want my employees to value education and be rewarded for their initiative when they want to learn. I've found it's money well spent.

I also ask employees what they want their compensation to be in three years. If they can reach that pay level in our company, we lay out a three-year plan for how they get there. If the compensation they want isn't possible in our company, we still lay out a plan with them but add the caveat they'll have to go somewhere else for that level of pay.

I might sound crazy for pointing my best employees

toward other companies, but I don't see it as crazy. My job is to get employees moving on an upward trajectory, so they're constantly improving and benefiting our company as they go. I can't predict where my employees will be in three years and neither can they, so I don't worry about it.

At the end of performance reviews, the employees and I identify areas of improvement and discuss specific check points that will let them know they're on the right track.

My son learned firsthand the value of specific feedback during his eighth grade year, when his football coach—a blunt, straightforward man—told me Tommy said all the right things but wasn't getting it done on the field. When I went home that day, I relayed the coach's message to Tommy and told him what my father once told me:

"Words come cheap. Performance is what matters."

I didn't have to say anything else.

Tommy's team won three state championships in football during his four years of high school, he was voted team captain his senior year, and received "Athlete of the Year" honors from his coaches. His football career turned around, because one coach had the guts to be honest about his performance.

If you take an honest approach to performance reviews, employee performance will turn around. I've only had a few instances where employees didn't work out, and the problem was usually them thinking they were bigger than the company. In situations like these, I pull out the policy and procedures manual that lays out employee expectations, point out which policy the offending party violated, and then show them the door.

Remember, though, if you do a good job with "you're hired," you rarely have to say, "you're fired." Performance reviews help with the times in between.

WHAT EMPLOYEES MOST WANT FROM OWNERS

This chapter has laid out the ways owners can take full advantage of their team. No other asset is more essential for improving the profitability of a business. That's why my first act as a new owner is calling a company-wide meeting that gets everyone involved. No other action initiates a turnaround faster than leveraging the team on day one.

In laying out the steps for owners to follow, we've also covered the qualities employees most desire from the owner—honesty and consistent communication about where the business is headed. Use regular meetings to update your team on the company's progress and leave time for questions. Encourage your employees to think about profitability and keep them focused on reducing expenses within their department.

As an owner, it's your job to kick any hurdles out the way so your employees can do their jobs well. If miscommunication is an issue, schedule lunch meetings. If your team lacks training, bring in someone to train them. If ineffective performance is hurting the company, work with your employees to see how they can improve moving forward.

In Chapter Six, we'll cover the qualities that make for a good business leader. The most important thing to understand is your team holds the key to your success. Treat them well, value their contributions, and push them to get better. You'll be glad you did.

Once the team is onboard, it's time to plan.

HAVE A PLAN

Every time I take over a struggling company, I'm reminded of the quote from T. Boone Pickens, one of my business heroes: "A fool with a plan can outsmart a genius with no plan." As I've said before, troubled businesses aren't started by fools, but by smart people who failed to plan, abandoned their plan, or overcomplicated things.

I've noticed telltale signs over the years of an owner's plan going awry. They blame external factors like uncooperative banks, increasing raw material costs, and market decline. If they just had more capital, their profits would surely go up.

Of course, the money they've already borrowed didn't strengthen their cash position or allow them to decrease their debt, but you can't tell them that. Slow payment of accounts payable, and an increase in accounts receivable, are also symptomatic of the real issue. When owners fail to plan, the company slowly slips into disarray.

When I call a company-wide meeting on day one in a new business, I lay out the truth, so every employee knows the baseline from which our turnaround will start. Good plans are rooted in clear communication, consistent execution, and continued evolution. I want my team to know exactly where we are and where we're headed.

A good plan tells you who's doing what to whom (job duties), when (timing), and for how much (cost). All these factors combined give your business forward momentum.

You can't get your team involved in the turnaround and fail to create a plan. Would you invite friends on a trip without telling them the destination, when you're leaving, how long the trip lasts, or what you'll be doing? I hope you're not that kind of friend!

Turning around an underperforming business is a journey filled with exciting possibilities and new challenges. Your plan is like a roadmap to help you navigate the ups and downs.

With that said, your employees probably won't be thrilled

to learn their role in putting together a ninety-day plan. Expect a lot of eye rolls and blank expressions at first, but once you explain you're looking for more of a football game plan than a Harvard business plan, employees tend to perk up and pay attention again.

With your team, you'll outline what needs to take place over the next ninety days to improve profitability, then break that down into thirty-day and weekly sections. You need to consider factors like debt, profit and loss information over the past few years, pricing, marketing efforts, financial controls, overhead, and customer value.

You must examine every aspect of your business through the lens of increasing profit. Far too few small and medium-sized companies have a profit culture. In our companies, I want everyone talking about profit, because nothing else unifies a team and gets them pulling in the same direction quicker than a better bottom line.

YOUR PLAN ONLY HAS TO BE GOOD ENOUGH

In the 1970s, I owned an engineering company that supplied high-tech equipment for marine oil and gas pipelines all over the world. At that time, British Petroleum (BP) was doing more pipeline work than any other company, and BP's Dr. Cotton was one of the world's leading experts on pipeline construction. Imagine the thrill I got when Dr. Cotton called asking if we'd bring our equipment to the UK for a demonstration.

We made the trip and I watched with growing excitement as Dr. Cotton circled the entire demonstration looking at all parts of the process. I knew we were about to hook the biggest fish in our world. When the demonstration ended, Dr. Cotton shook my hand and said, "I'm impressed with your company's equipment, and the team you've got."

Hot damn, I thought. We'd done it. We'd landed BP as a client.

"So, you're going to use our equipment, Dr. Cotton?" I asked.

I remember his answer to this day: "Oh, no. What we have is good enough."

Good enough. I found meaning in those words beyond what Dr. Cotton intended.

Too often, companies are obsessed with perfection. Valuable time and money is wasted chasing something to the 100th percentile when getting to 80%, or good enough, would suffice. Your company's plan only needs to be good enough at the start, so don't waste time trying to make it perfect. You'll update it every week with your team.

Your main goal starting out is to get all the employees thinking along the same lines.

GROWING A BUSINESS WITHOUT A PLAN LEADS TO DISASTER

You would think, because I buy businesses in trouble, they've all been in decline.

Wrong!

Every business I've bought has been in a growth mode, yet none of them had a plan. In my mind, that's like trying to drive a Ferrari down a curvy road at 170 miles per hour at night without headlights. You might stay on the road for a while, but eventually you're going to crash.

Without a plan, you can't anticipate problems. You're constantly in reactionary mode, putting out one fire only for another one to flare up. You can prevent fires, rather than putting them out, if you plan for the challenges of growth. Yet, I've seen seventy-seven owners who lost their company, because they preferred to fly by the seat of their pants.

One such owner ran a company that manufactured custom

equipment. About a year before I bought the company, they received a massive order from their best customer. Without any planning, the owner made an addition to his plant, purchased over a million dollars worth of new equipment, and hired many new employees.

As you might expect, the results were disastrous. The owner couldn't adequately train the new staff within the tight order fulfillment window. His overhead soared, he didn't prepare accounting for higher accounts payable, and the company's cash flow dried up. Like the Ferrari driver going 170 mph down the curvy road, the company crashed.

Out-of-control growth creates weak links within your company. At the worst possible time, when you're under enormous pressure, that weak link is going to snap. It doesn't have to be this way, though. Due to their size, small and medium-sized businesses can quickly adapt their plan to deal with external factors. With an adaptable plan, you leave nothing to chance. You're controlling your circumstances, not the other way around.

TO CHANGE YOUR PLAN, CONSULT WITH YOUR TEAM

After a few weeks with a plan, everyone will understand how departments within the company function and relate to one another. As a result, you're going to see immediate improvement. When your business is underperforming, taking that first step in the right direction is an amazing moment that re-energizes your whole team.

The way to keep taking those steps forward is to update your plan every week. In our companies, we update our plan on Friday mornings. I do this for two reasons:

1. To give us a clear vision for what needs to be done the following week.
2. To reiterate to everyone our plan is the driving force in the company.

I want our plan fresh on everyone's minds when they leave Friday afternoon, so it's the first thing they remember when they come in Monday morning. If you fail to update the plan, you'll undermine its legitimacy and your commitment to turning things around.

As we've discussed, meetings should be short and to the point. After a few weeks, it should take ten minutes to answer the following questions: How did we do this week versus the plan? How do we need to adjust for next week? What unanticipated problems popped up? Does everybody know what they're doing next week?

Weekly updates help you identify the weak areas of your

company and let you focus on improving those areas. This isn't rocket science—problem areas will be obvious when you're tracking against your plan. As you seek ways to improve, I'll reiterate a lesson from Chapter Two: Listen to your team. Be open to ideas you've never tried before. After all, you won't know if they work until you try them out.

In one of the manufacturing companies I owned, our tool and die department was slowing down our production time. One of the operators suggested during a weekly meeting that we reach out to another tool and die shop across town.

"They don't have much work right now," he said. "Could they help us catch up?"

I had never considered such a solution, but while the rest of the team continued to work on the plan, I went to my office and called the owner of the other shop. Within ten minutes, we made a deal to help each other. It was a win-win for both companies: He didn't have to lay off his workers, and we could catch up with their help. When we had slow times in the future, we did work for him under the same arrangement.

When I went back to the meeting and shared the news,

the operator beamed with pride, along with everyone else. They realized in that moment good ideas don't have to come from the owner or managers. They can and should come from the guys down in the trenches. Had it not been for his idea, I probably would've bought more equipment and hired more staff (a solution too familiar and not the best route).

As owners, we sometimes operate with tunnel vision. When your team meets weekly to discuss changes, they can bring fresh ideas that wouldn't otherwise be on your radar.

THE PARTS OF A GOOD PLAN

A good plan starts with a simple focus: making a profit.

Somewhere along the way, society developed this idea that it's poor taste for companies to admit they want to make money. As a business owner, I want to make a lot of money for myself and my team. As a fellow business owner, you should place a similar priority on profit. You can have other goals, of course, but if you don't make profitability the goal of your company, you won't be in business long enough to achieve your other goals. As the famous economist John Kenneth Galbraith said, "Without the short term there is no long term."

We know our ninety-day plan will be broken down into thirty-day increments, which will then be broken down into weekly plans. All three iterations should include the following:

- Where the company is right now
    - The baseline discussed in your first company-wide meeting
- Where the company is headed
    - Projected revenue for the next ninety days, thirty days, and the next week
- How we're going to get there
    - Start by reducing expenses across the entire company
    - Implement suggestions from the team
    - Modify improvement strategies each week to see what works best
- How every employee fits into this plan
    - Who is doing what to whom, when, and for how much
    - Make sure everyone understands their role
    - Include metrics that let employees quantify their performance

Simple, right? In Chapter Four, we'll dive into how you measure your results to see if the company is on track, but drawing up the initial plan is not a complex task.

The baseline should include the balance of your bank accounts and the money in accounts payable and receivable. As Dr. Cotton said, you're looking for "good enough." Don't stress your accountant out—get within $5,000 and move forward with the plan.

As part of expense reduction, call your vendors to discuss new terms.

If payment is due in thirty days, see if they'll extend it to sixty days, thereby improving your cash flow. Also, if you're buying products in bulk quantities every thirty days and putting them in inventory, see if the vendor will let you buy them on an as-needed basis. My experience has been vendors are willing to work with you, if you'll just ask (we'll revisit this topic in more depth in Chapter Five).

You should also discuss the ongoing needs of the company during the planning phase. The owners whose companies I've taken over withheld financial information because they didn't want employees demanding raises if the company made a profit. The best way to head that discussion off before it begins is to confront the following questions:

- How much debt do we have to pay off?
- Do we need to purchase new equipment or hire new employees?

- What are the marketing costs we'll incur to increase sales?
- How much cash do we need in reserve as failure insurance?

The answers to these questions belong in your plan, and by discussing them with your team, you're teaching them higher profit does not equate to higher salaries. When you explain you're thinking about the company's long-term success, they'll understand. Plus, if you implement the alternative to raises we'll cover in the next chapter, your employees can still enjoy a portion of the profit they helped bring in.

YOUR REVENUE GOALS SHOULD BE REALISTIC

Honesty is a huge asset when you're projecting revenue for your plan. If your company has gross sales of $100,000 a week, there's no magic wand you can wave to increase sales to $200,000 by next week. Look at the limitations you have in place and correct them, but understand realistic revenue numbers are vital to your plan.

If you aim too high and fall miserably short of your goal, morale is going to be crushed. Talk with your team and let them provide you with the information needed to make an accurate projection of where revenue can go within ninety days. Aim for steady, achievable growth that encourages the team and gives you time to adjust your plan each week.

Then again, you might project little or no revenue increase in your first ninety-day plan if your business is really struggling. Like we discussed in Chapter Two, companies in bad shape should focus less on increasing revenue and more on decreasing expenses at first. If you keep revenue where it is and decrease expense, you're still improving profitability.

Although it sounds counterintuitive to planning, remember you shouldn't put a number on expense reduction. Challenge your team to cut costs at the first meeting and check in every week to see how much fat your team has trimmed.

However, if your team wants to set a goal for reducing expenses, encourage them if you think the goal is realistic. Keep in mind the companies I took over always cut at least 34% of our expenses, so if I were you, I'd be comfortable with any goal under 50%.

Review all reductions with your team to make sure they're cutting non-essential items. Sometimes the desire to reach a goal can outweigh common sense, and employees will cut essential components of the business to cross the threshold they set. Ask your team to make sensible, intelligent cuts, to use a scalpel and not an axe.

Regardless of your starting point, your plan should initiate company-wide change. You can't accept a "business as usual" mentality. I'm willing to bet, you picked up this book because you know your business needs help in ways big or small. I also understand change is difficult in any part of our lives, so I say to you: Start small and grow.

Humans tend to overestimate what we can do in a short time and underestimate what we can do over a long period. Set an attainable goal for the first ninety days, but don't sell yourself short long term. You'll be amazed at what a motivated team can accomplish.

Once your first plan runs its course, create a new one. If you didn't project a revenue increase in your first plan, you might look at ways to increase revenue the next ninety days. If you're not ready, keep striving toward that goal and you'll get there sooner than you think.

As you build a new plan every ninety days, you'll find you can add more complex information into each successive plan than you had in previous versions. This goes back to the value of learning—once employees understand the basic information in your first plan, they'll become comfortable with adding more variables to the equation.

EVERY BUSINESS NEEDS AN ORGANIZATIONAL CHART

In addition to a plan, your business also needs an organizational chart. It doesn't matter if you have four employees or 400—you need one. I say this for a few reasons, the first of which is an org chart is a tool of growth. You might have four employees now, but when your company grows, and you're hiring new folks, you need a structure in place to ensure you're adding people to the right seats at the right time.

Disorganization and miscommunication are two problems that submarine business growth, and you're inviting those problems into your business if you grow without an org chart.

If you're saying to yourself, "I have an org chart. I'm good to go," let me ask you this: When was the last time you updated that chart? If you don't continue building that structure as your business grows, your org chart is nothing but a useless relic.

Org charts also assuage bankers' fears when you ask them for a loan. They're worried about what I call the "Mack

Truck Theory" of business: If you're the only person who is knowledgeable about the workings of your business, and you step off the curb and get hit by a Mack truck tomorrow, that business and the bank are in deep trouble.

An org chart shows lenders your company is organized and not centered on one person. Should you tragically perish, repayment of the loan could still happen.

Business growth allows owners to hire managers who can handle tasks the owner used to handle. Instead of twenty people reporting to him, now the owner has a team of managers he communicates with daily. An org chart helps everyone understand the breakdown of authority and keeps owners from undermining their managers.

I've watched, in companies with several hundred employees, the owner rush out of his office and go four levels down the org chart to ask an employee a question or give that employee a task to complete. Those owners undermined the authority of their managers by going around them, instead of going through them to the employee.

Furthermore, what happens if the employee got different marching orders from their manager? They're now stuck with a difficult decision: Do what their manager says, or do what the owner says.

Don't confuse your employees or undermine your managers. Respect the org chart and empower your team to do their jobs without you having to micromanage everything.

Having an org chart also helps you know when to hire new managers. You get to a point of diminishing returns when it comes to the number of people reporting to a certain manager. If any of your leaders are overwhelmed, use the org chart to see where a new position could be added and which employees would report to that person.

Finally, sit down with your vendors and go over your org chart with them. It saves time when vendors direct their questions to the right people at your company.

YOU DON'T NEED TO BE A ROCKET SCIENTIST

Early in this book, I promised you meat and potatoes solutions to the problems facing your business. I'm not interested in sharing big words or fancy theories. If what we've covered in this chapter seems too simplistic, I'll remind you of a lesson from Chapter One:

Business is only complicated if you make it that way.

The components of a good business plan might seem ordinary, but I promise if you'll commit to implementing them, you'll see extraordinary results. I've used this approach seventy-seven times in a variety of businesses over five decades. It's worked every single time.

I didn't need Harvard business plans to build profitable companies and neither do you. All you need are a few timeless business principles and your common sense.

In other words, you don't need to be a rocket scientist.

The first three ingredients of a turnaround are 1. a simple approach, 2. the support of your team, and 3. a plan to be your guiding light. These three elements lay the foundation.

Now that you've built the foundation, it's time to implement a system that lets you know if your plan is working. To do this, we need to turn on your headlights.

TURN ON YOUR
HEADLIGHTS

Traditional accounting methods are holding your business back. Think about it like this:

You arrive late to a basketball game and don't see a score on the scoreboard. You turn to the person sitting next to you and ask for the score.

"They're not keeping score," the person responds.

"How much time is left?" you ask.

"They're not keeping a game clock, either," comes the reply.

"Then, how do we know what's going on in the game?" you ask, frustrated.

The person merely shrugs and resumes watching the pointless game.

While this sounds like a bizarre scenario, 99% of businesses operate by these rules, when it comes to accounting. If you walked through the doors of any business and asked the owner about his company's financial state at that moment, he wouldn't have an answer. He might know where he's been, but he's got no clue where he is, or where he's going.

Most small and medium-sized businesses use taillight accounting to look backward at their financial situation thirty or sixty days ago. Owners use P&L reports, balance sheets, and cash flow statements to measure against previous months or against this time last year. Taillight accounting and reflecting over the past month is no doubt important.

However, there are flaws with this idea of "looking back to look forward."

For one, P&L reports usually come with a lag time of ten to twelve days, as various accounts are reconciled. If the banks and any outside accounting firms you use are on top of things, you're lucky to get your January P&L by February 10. By then, you're forty-one days removed from the beginning of the month you're reviewing.

Most business owners would shrug at such a delay. What's the big deal, right?

Imagine how much trouble you'd be in if your bookkeeper made a mistake on January 1 and repeated it forty times, before you caught it on February 10. Think of the dread you'd feel if revenue declined in December and January's P&L confirmed your fear the slide would continue. By then, your turnaround attempt is six weeks behind.

Taillight accounting is also flawed because it represents a snapshot in time. January's P&L report might show you had a good month. What that snapshot might not show is an invoice received January 20 that was net 10 (due in ten days). Instead of paying it and showing a loss for the month, the bookkeeper buried it and paid in February.

Suddenly, the rosy picture painted by January's report looks a little bleaker.

While important, taillight accounting does not accurately convey where businesses stand or give owners the information they need to guide their business moving forward.

Think back to the Ferrari from Chapter Three, only now picture you're driving down a curvy road in the dead of night with no headlights to guide you. The only illumination on this treacherous path is your taillights. How long can you drive before crashing?

Business is no different. When you don't know where you are, or where you're going, you strip away your ability to change directions and avoid certain disaster.

To keep your business from going off the cliff, we need to turn on your headlights.

WHAT IS YOUR TRUE MEASURE OF SUCCESS?

The first step in headlight accounting is to identify what you must measure to know if your business is succeeding or failing. For example, we own apartment complexes. Every day, I receive a DOC (daily operating control) sheet from those complexes. Here are the metrics we look at on those DOC sheets:

- Number of vacant apartment units
- Number of approved credit deposits
- Number of tenants with past-due rent
- Number of expiring leases for the next four months

We've learned over the years that these metrics give us the best indication of where we are, and where we're headed in the coming months. With this information, our headlights shine bright and illuminate the way forward. If we have forty leases expiring in the next four months, our team at the facility can be proactive and call residents to find out their status and offer them exemption from rent increases if they extend their lease.

On the flip side, if we have no expiring leases in January, and our team has renewed everyone who's expiring in February, we can back off on advertising those two months, since we don't have any available units. Using our headlights saves us money.

To help you visualize what I'm talking about, look at the top half of the six-month DOC board we have in the office at our apartment complex:

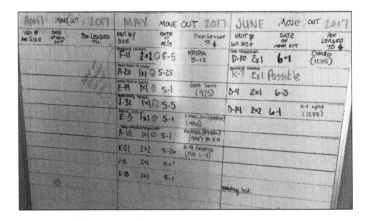

This board shows both move-out and move-in dates for pre-approved residents in April, May, and June, as these apartments will be top priority for our maintenance team. Visit robertthomasbethel.com for more examples of DOC boards we use in our businesses.

You must decide what metric is the best barometer of your success. It could be number of units produced, clients booked, products sold, or contracts renewed. When it comes down to it, how is your business ultimately making its money? You can have more than one metric, but there are two important points to consider here:

1. Your metrics should be clearly defined—revenue, expenses, etc.
2. Your metrics should be easy for your team to pull together.

Owners should be able to glance at a DOC sheet and know where their business stands on that day. At the same time, team members shouldn't spend hours assembling this report. It takes five minutes to put together the DOC sheets for our apartments.

Once you decide what method of measurement best suits your business, your next step is to purchase those whiteboards I mentioned in the introduction. You're going to chart the DOC sheet information on the whiteboards and place them somewhere employees can see them easily, be it a hallway or break room. Don't hide them in the accounting office.

Here's an example of what your chart might look like:

MONTH GOAL 850 UNITS

In this example, you have a manufacturing company that knows from its ninety-day plan it needs to sell 850 units this month. Over twenty operating days, that's 42.5 units per day.

Every day, someone from accounting is going to update this board with the volume sold in the past twenty-four hours. Those daily updates show if the company is on target, below target, or above target. (In our companies, we update the board between 2-3 pm and have the same person do it every day.) There's no need for meetings or memos from the owner—employees can see the company's progress always.

You might need five boards in your company depending on how many metrics you identify. The important point is to place them where everyone can see them. Simple as they may seem, whiteboards are the most effective tool I've found for driving people toward the goal we set forth in our ninety-day plan. Not only do they keep the company on track, they provide the best form of silent motivation. If you're ahead of target, everybody will be excited, but if you're below, everybody will bust ass to get above the target line.

As the owner, you don't have to say a word.

A THIRTY-DAY MINDSET IS VITAL TO PROFITABILITY

The DOC sheet is your most effective tool when it comes to daily operations. A P&L report is an important piece of historical data to have and study, but when so much can happen outside that thirty-day snapshot before you see the report, you can't rely on a P&L to be the guiding force inside your company. You can't look forward with just your taillights.

Charting your daily progress on whiteboards creates a thirty-day mentality that is a powerful force for profitability in your company. Very few companies I've taken over understood the importance of acquiring profit in thirty-day chunks.

One exception is car dealerships, which must report their sales to a manufacturer on a monthly basis. Dealerships will run internal contests to motivate their salespeople and ensure they hit their monthly sales total.

If you need to buy a new car, go the last two or three days of the month when dealerships are highly motivated to get every sale they can. You'll find great deals!

Dealerships demonstrate two reasons a thirty-day mindset is vital to a profit-minded culture:

1. The biggest potential for profit increase occurs within a thirty-day window.
2. Employees should take it up a level at month's end to hit the sales goal.

Every company has fixed expenses like rent, utilities, other overhead items, and payroll. Each month, revenue from your sales goes to pay off those expenses until those costs are covered. That is the breakeven point. Once that happens, your team should kick things into high gear and pile as much revenue into the remaining time as possible, because you're accumulating a much higher level of profit.

Employees shouldn't act the same on the first day of the month versus the twentieth day if you create a profit-minded culture in your company. As the owner, help your team see why a thirty-day mindset is the fastest path to improved profitability. When you hit the point during the first thirty-day window where your expenses are covered (breakeven), congratulate the team in your weekly meeting and encourage them to finish strong the rest of the month.

Set that expectation at the outset, and you won't need to remind them what's expected when the month is drawing to a close. Armed with just a thirty-day mindset and a few whiteboards, your team can become a lean, mean, profit-making machine.

INSTEAD OF RAISES, GIVE OUT BONUSES

One of the biggest fears business owners share with me is

employees asking for raises if the company makes more money. For most owners who don't share financial information with employees, that fear is the primary reason why. On the flip side, owners are afraid employees will leave if profits decline.

We covered in Chapter Two why the second fear—employees leaving—is baseless. As for employees demanding their share of new profits, here's a one-word solution: bonuses.

My goal when I take over a new company is to increase profitability, so I address this issue with my employees during our first meeting. I share that I want every employee to make more money doing this job here than they could anywhere within one hundred miles (I limit it to one hundred miles because someone could take a job in New York and make more money).

I want everyone to understand my goal is for them to make as much money as we can pay them. Once that fact is established, I add the caveat that raises will no longer be part of the compensation plan. Instead, we're going to give bonuses.

Let's look at an example that explains why bonuses are preferable to raises.

Say you own a company with one hundred employees, and you make good profit. To reward your team's hard work, you give everyone a 5% raise on January 1. After another good year, you give a second 5% raise on January 1 the following year.

Within thirteen months (January 1 to January 31 of the next year, once everyone is paid their new salary), you've rewarded past performance with a 10% payroll increase.

If you haven't increased your prices to match your higher operating expense—something no owner I've spoken with has done, since it might price them out of the market—that 10% increase cuts into your profitability. Worse yet, you've raised expenses going into an unknown future with zero idea of how profitable you'll be. You're assuming the good times will keep on rolling because they have in the past, but that's a dangerous game to play. Ask any of the owners whose businesses I've bought, and they'll all tell you the same thing: Past performance is not an indicator of future results.

We pay out bonuses on December 31 in all but three of our companies, and in those companies, we do quarterly bonuses. I made the mistake once of implementing monthly bonuses and found out my team threw expenses into the next month, so their bonus checks would be fatter. We suffered a huge loss the next month when all the deferred expenses were paid, and that was the end of monthly bonuses for me.

Much like expense cutting, I don't attach a percentage to our bonuses, but I can tell you the employees of our companies are happy with the bonuses they receive.

Annual bonuses are paid out from the money you made during the year and don't increase your operating costs heading into the new year. Make sure your employees understand bonuses allow you to protect the best interests of the company. Bonuses don't mortgage your future. Raises do. Besides, if the average wage increase is 2–3%, and the bonus ends up being 15–18%, employees are getting a much sweeter deal.

As one of my business partners put it once, "We're all on commission, most of us just don't know it." Even if an employee is salaried, that salary is only guaranteed if the company makes money. Giving that person a raise isn't worth much, if profits dry up and the company goes bankrupt. Using bonuses to reward performance reduces the chance of that happening.

HOW MUCH DOES IT COST TO OPEN YOUR DOORS?

Headlight accounting is about seizing control of the

factors that influence your profitability. As business owners, we do this through meaningful measurement, daily tracking, and the continued education of ourselves and our employees.

So far, we've talked about a thirty-day mindset and bonuses over raises, but expenses are another area to consider.

If it's the end of the month and you're way below the line on your whiteboard, you better pump the brakes on spending to increase your chances of making a profit that month (or at least breaking even). However, it's not fair to ask that of your team, if you didn't show them the company's monthly expenses up front. Sure, they can rein in spending, but they're not going to understand why it's a necessary move, which leads to frustration.

In the average company, the employees can't tell you what it costs to open the doors of the business every day. Hell, most owners don't even know that number! I've asked that question of both parties over the years, and I've gotten blank stares more times than I can count. Headlight accounting demands everyone know about expenses, so let's crack open the books and figure out together what it costs to run your business.

Add up fixed expenses like rent and insurance to get

your first monthly sum. Then, find the average of variable expenses like utilities, payroll (if you have hourly employees), and cost of materials over the past twelve months. If you recently added new expense by purchasing new equipment or hiring employees, factor those costs into your calculations. Add the averages of each variable expense together, then add in your fixed cost sum.

While not exact (but good enough), you now have an approximation of your monthly expenses, and when you divide that cost by the number of days you operate within a thirty-day window, you've got your daily operating cost, or what it cost to open the doors each day.

I can promise you, from fifty-two years of experience, when you share that daily cost with your team, their jaws will drop. It gives them a new appreciation for being able to work where they do and reinforces a thirty-day mindset. They'll understand why the goal is to cover expenses as quickly as possible and stockpile profit.

Opening the books, while scary, allows owners to exploit human nature. Like a runner's kick at the end of a race, employees will take things up a notch once overhead is covered. Think about it—wouldn't you want to pour as much money into the company as possible if you knew a portion of that profit was coming back to you as a bonus?

If your employees don't know your monthly expenses or understand the importance of a thirty-day mindset, you can't leverage the innate competitiveness of your team.

IMPLEMENT A PURCHASE ORDER SYSTEM AND SIGN ALL CHECKS YOURSELF

The best way business owners can control expenses is to get in front of the process. If you wait to come in at the end, it's too late—those costs are going to get paid.

I once sat in a CEO's office and watched as the accountant brought in a stack of checks for him to sign. The accountant had done an excellent job providing backup documentation and invoices, in case the CEO had questions. Yet, when the CEO arrived at one check, his brow furrowed and his eyes narrowed. He pointed at the check and said with all the confidence in the world, "I'm not paying this," like by saying it, he could make it true.

The only thought going through my mind was, "Oh yes, you are going to pay it."

For whatever bravado the CEO showed in his office, someone in his company obligated him to pay whatever cost he was refusing to pay. If he'd been out in front of the process, he could have stopped the expense if he felt it unnecessary or excessive. Instead, he was left holding a bill so egregious, it inspired his amusing (but hollow) threat.

You can use purchase order (PO) books to take back control of your company's spending. Get a PO book for each department, and when employees write up a PO for vendors, send copies to accounting. If a PO is above a certain threshold you set, make it so the department manager, accountant, and owner must sign off on it.

We implemented this stipulation in our companies, not to override anybody or interfere with operations, but to keep all decision makers in the loop on spending.

Returning to our example, had the CEO been signing off on expensive purchase orders, he could have discussed the expense before he was obligated to pay it. If he looked at the revenue whiteboard and saw the company was below its monthly goal, he could've rejected the PO or deferred it until the timing made sense for the company.

Timing of accounts payable is critical to cash flow management. An owner's biggest job is to coordinate all departments to ensure cash flow always remains healthy. I've learned ill-timed expenses dry up cash flow faster than anything else. When a purchase order comes across your desk, ask yourself these questions:

- Do we need this now?
- What kind of billing can we get?
- Can we negotiate better terms?

I've taken over businesses that had zero cash flow, where accountants brought me checks to sign on invoices that weren't due for another twenty days. Some vendors provide discounts for paying early, but we weren't able to worry about that perk. When I asked the accountant why the check was sent out in advance, I got a shrug and this half-baked rationale: "I was caught up and thought I'd send out some checks."

When I say owners must educate employees on how a profitable business operates, stories like this one explain my reasoning. Your employees aren't stupid. They're not trying to intentionally submarine the company that signs their paychecks. Most of them simply lack an understanding of basic business principles. It's your job to teach them.

This story also reinforces the idea owners should sign every check their business writes. There are two main reasons why signing checks is good practice.

First, it allows you to put your final stamp of approval on spending. Second, checks allow you to see where you're spending money. When you see repetitive invoices enough, you get a sense for when a certain cost rises and can decide if you should bid out that service.

You'll be surprised at what sticks in your mind when you're signing checks.

YOU PROBABLY NEED TO RETHINK YOUR ACCOUNTS RECEIVABLE

When I was in my twenties, we received a line of company credit. A few days later, I was at the bank and saw the chairman of the board, who was a friend of my parents, and although I figured he knew nothing about the line of credit, I thanked him. Quite to my surprise, he said, "I need you to do something for me. I'll stay out of your business, if you'll stay out of my business."

I died laughing because I had no interest in getting in the banking business and told him as much. With a straight face, he replied, "Bob, you're already in the banking business."

"What do you mean?" I asked him.

"You have accounts receivable on your books," he

explained. "What that means is you're borrowing money from our bank to loan to your customers."

His words hit me like a ton of bricks. I'd never thought about it, but he was right.

When customers bought our products, we sent out net-30 invoices. While that statement sat out there, we continued to pay our expenses. So, where did the money come from that allowed the customer to purchase our product? It came from the bank, through our company.

Have you ever thought about the impact accounts receivable has on your bottom line?

Let me give you an example: Say you sell a product to Josh's company for $1,000. Your cost on that product is $800, so your profit margin is $200. When you send out the invoice to Josh's company, you're shocked to learn his operation has gone bankrupt.

Here's where the real problems begin.

Not only have you covered expenses waiting for this invoice to be paid, but now you've lost your profit and you're out of pocket for the product. Because you're an unsecured creditor, you might get back five cents on the dollar from Josh, but there's no way you'll get the full $1,000. Now, you've got to sell four more products to cover the loss of Josh's sale.

Years ago, I met a fellow business owner who learned the hard way not to carry accounts receivable. We were doing rehab on a commercial building and came to the man's building supply company to set up an account for $600,000 worth of material.

As we talked, I noticed he accepted American Express, and I asked if that applied to large purchases like ours. "Sure, why not?" he said, which surprised me considering the fee he'd have to pay to American Express on $600,000 worth of business.

I learned that during a recent housing boom in this small Kentucky town, the owner had been carrying the business of local builders on net-30 accounts and borrowing money from the bank to cover his receivables. Everything was smooth until the largest builder in the area went bankrupt, leaving the business supply owner with hundreds of thousands in unpaid receivables. He told me it took him ten years to recover.

"American Express can't charge me enough to make me carry accounts receivable ever again," he said. "Every night, I go to sleep knowing all my money is in the bank."

I share these examples to emphasize this simple truth: Small and medium-sized businesses should not be in the business of loaning money.

Some of you may read that and say, "Our business can't get rid of accounts receivable!"

I'm here to tell you: Yes, you can.

Instead of running your own accounts receivable, turn those invoices over to a bank and let them factor your receivables for you. When companies owe money to a bank instead of your business, they tend to get serious about payment. Sure, the bank is going to charge you a handling fee, but I'd rather have 95% of the money I'm owed than 0%.

Hiccups with the payment of accounts receivable shouldn't be your problem. If you've got a stack of past-due invoices on your desk, you're killing your cash flow.

Headlight accounting depends on knowing where you stand always.

Accounts receivable create a cash flow mystery that dims your headlights and makes it impossible for you to know where you're headed. You can guess, but until those invoices are paid, you're simply crossing your fingers and hoping for the best.

Remember our path to profitability is paved with certainty, not ambiguity.

CLEAR OUT INVENTORY ON A YEARLY BASIS

Headlight accounting also involves clearing out your inventory each year. If you're familiar with inventory accounting, you probably recognize these terms:

FIFO: First In, First Out

LIFO: Last In, First Out

There are arguments to be made for either system, but the premise is with FIFO, the original cost is maintained, while with LIFO, the price may have been reduced, so you want to average out. Whatever your preference, I came to realize there is a third inventory system as well:

FISH: First In, Still Here

I've come across very few inventories throughout the years that were fresh. Old products that weren't sold and couldn't be sent back to the manufacturer were crammed onto shelves gathering dust in multiple companies I took over. Yet, when I looked at the books, those companies were carrying the original value of that obsolete inventory, which inflated their value well beyond what those companies were reasonably worth.

One company I considered buying had $100,000 worth of obsolescence in an inventory worth $300,000. When I asked the owner why he hadn't sold the obsolete inventory to get it off his books and make a little bit of money, his answer demonstrated three fears most owners share about getting rid of FISH inventory:

- Fear #1: The company won't get much for the obsolete inventory.
- Fear #2: Selling it would reduce equity in the company.
- Fear #3: A reduction in equity might cause problems with the bank.

I certainly understand those fears, but I've learned through experience that they're unfounded. When I take over a company with FISH inventory, I clear it out as soon as I can, because I'm not interested in puffing up my value for the banks. If you have FISH inventory on your books, you need to stop lying to yourself.

Take your obsolete inventory—anything that hasn't moved

in a year—and get what you can for it now. Sell it on eBay or contact a surplus inventory buyer. Moving forward, make it a priority to keep a clean inventory. When you shelve excess equipment or products, it will meet one or more of these fates—broken, lost, or covered in dust.

All three endings add zero value to your company. Depending on the size of your facility, FISH inventory also makes your space look junky and dirty, which leaves visitors with a poor impression of your business, be they customers, lenders, or investors.

Here are a couple of strategies you can use to keep your inventory clean.

First, resist the temptation to buy large quantities of products for the price break. If you only need 500 of something, don't order 1,000, because it's a "better deal." Whatever value you receive on the front end chasing price breaks will be lost when those 500 products you didn't use are crammed on a shelf somewhere.

Second, talk with your vendors about as-needed terms. If you're using a component every week for the foreseeable future, contact the supplier and ask if they'll carry the inventory and let you order the part as needed. If they agree, you've just improved your cash flow by reducing the size of your invoices and saved yourself from FISH inventory.

As an owner, remember you only reap these benefits if you get in front of this process and educate your purchasing department on the questions they should ask.

If you're not the one making it happen, it's not going to happen.

WHEN IT COMES TO ACCOUNTING AND LAW FIRMS, BIGGER IS BETTER

We've spent this chapter talking about headlight accounting within your company and what that looks like, but you're also going to need the services of a good accounting firm. Some small businesses prefer to work with one or two-person accounting offices, and that's fine. During fifty-two years, I've seen the benefits of working with large national firms and would recommend utilizing their services over those offered by local accountants.

The first benefit of working with a well-known firm is credibility with lenders. When banks know they'll be getting monthly financials from a top national CPA firm, they can rest assured that your business is being looked after.

Large firms also house accountants specializing in

whatever field of accounting you need: tax work, estate planning, auditing, etc.

The small accounting office down the street can't offer you those benefits. In fact, some of the international companies I've dealt with over the years wouldn't recognize accounting from local CPAs, no matter how exceptional their work. The work had to come from one of the large accounting firms they recognized and trusted. In addition, if you do any cost-plus work, your client and your lender may require a national firm if they require an annual audit. Fair or not, that is the reality.

You'll pay more to work with a national firm, but I've learned over the years that having their help when you need it saves you more money than you spend.

One thing you shouldn't expect of any accounting firm, regardless of size, is for them to help run your business. I've seen countless owners make this costly mistake. Accountants can advise you on generally accepted accounting practices (GAAP), crunch numbers if you're considering a new investment, and offer their professional advice.

However, you shouldn't expect or want your accountants to make business decisions for you. For the most part, accountants come out of school and go straight into practice. Most of them have never run a business or been trained in best business practices. Remember, if you have a CPA firm pulling your monthly P&L, they are simply recording history.

You need to leverage the expertise accountants have in their field and make your own decisions. No outside entity knows better than you what's best for your business, and as such, you should educate your accountants on the finer points of your business. The better they understand what you're doing, the better equipped they are to notice when some part of your business is out of whack and requires your attention.

The same logic applies to law firms. Today's businesses need to work with a national law firm that has the staff to cover all aspects of legal issues. As with national CPA firms, lenders are more comfortable if you are working with a national law firm. Over the years, the companies I have owned have been represented by some excellent attorneys with great law firms, including: John B. Connally III of Baker & Botts in Houston; Sid Nurkin of Powell, Goldstein, Frazer & Murphy in Atlanta; Larry Papel, managing partner of Nelson Mullins Riley & Scarborough in Nashville.

HEADLIGHT ACCOUNTING IS AN ONGOING EFFORT

As we wrap things up, remember headlight accounting will be as effective as you make it. If you update the whiteboards, reinforce the thirty-day mindset, use PO books to stay on top of daily expenditures, maintain a clean inventory, and utilize the services of national accounting firms and law firms, you will see massive improvement within your business.

I've applied these principles in seventy-seven companies and seen it work every single time.

If you continue to rely on your taillights, or even worse, get overconfident and shut off your headlights once you see some results, you're eventually going to crash.

That is not my opinion. It's an absolute certainty.

Turn your headlights on and leave them on. Once you're comfortable with that step, it's time to explore the next phase of business turnaround: cutting expenses.

CUT EXPENSES
TO PROSPER

The reason I've been able to help turn around so many businesses during the past fifty-two years is because of a universal truth—profit determines success or failure.

I've made a lot of money off the words, "But you don't understand, my business is different." No, friend, your business is exactly like every other.

It doesn't matter your industry, location, size, corporate setup, mission, or whatever—if your revenue doesn't exceed your expenses, you'll eventually crash and burn.

Even non-profits must worry about profit. After all, if they're not raising money, they're eventually going to collapse. Having a passion to help others is beautiful and important, but as that old song "Money, Money" from the musical *Cabaret* reminds us:

"Money makes the world go round."

So, whenever banks call me in, and I research a potential business, I start by looking at expenses. Almost always, they exceed the company's revenue. My next question is whether reducing costs can bring the business back from the brink. Sometimes, the business is too far underwater to be saved.

Unlike some consultants, I'm not interested in stepping into a new business with an axe and hacking away at expenses. I find that approach doesn't work long term.

I want to know if I recruit the employees to help me and take a surgeon's approach to trimming away small areas of wasteful spending, can we turn things around?

If the answer is yes, then I sign on and begin the process we've thus far described. Up until now, we've touched on the importance of expense reduction and control. In this chapter, we're going to dive deep into controlling expenses and what that looks like across the board.

We are not going to cover specific expenses for each

industry. If you want a better idea of what your monthly costs should be, connect with a successful owner in your industry and pick their brain, or do a simple Google search. The answers are out there.

We are going to cover the foundational pieces every successful business is built upon. Essentially, if you're not practicing what we cover in this chapter, you need to get started right away. I'm going to share some harsh truths, starting with this doozy:

You are most likely your company's single biggest expense.

YOUR MINDSET IS COSTING YOUR COMPANY MONEY

Years ago, I was called in by multiple banks to look at a large manufacturing plant with an owner who loved to flaunt his wealth. He lived in a million-dollar mansion, owned a huge houseboat, and wore $3,000 suits. The company paid for a pair of matching Mercedes for him and his wife, plus it covered the expenses on his Clearwater Beach condo. Unsurprisingly, he was also taking a huge salary.

One day, while I was visiting the plant, this owner called a company-wide meeting inside the large manufacturing bay. With roughly 200 of his loyal employees spread out on the floor below him, this guy walked out and lambasted the company's out-of-control expenses. To top it all off, he made this appalling proclamation:

"If you all don't start making a profit, I'm going to lose everything!"

You could almost see the steam rising from the heads of those employees, because they knew he was by far the company's biggest expense. Do you think any of them were foolish enough to point the finger back at that owner?

Of course not! They needed their paycheck, so they kept quiet.

I don't expect that any of you reading this are that tone deaf. I share that story to drive home the point that being a business owner requires constant self-reflection and a healthy dose of humility. A good place to start is with your salary. If you were to go into the marketplace to hire someone to replace you, what would you pay them?

If you can be replaced by someone making $100,000 a year, and you're paying yourself $500,000 annually, you're sucking away $400,000 in working capital and doing a huge disservice to your business. You need to be highly profitable, extremely efficient, and have a large cash reserve built up before you start paying yourself big bucks.

Don't fall into the trap of thinking the business owes you. Countless owners have trotted out that line over the years, and it's nothing but a steaming pile of BS.

Think of your business as a six-month-old baby. If you've ever called your business your "baby" at some point, this isn't too much of a stretch. With that mindset in place, would you ever tell someone a six-month-old baby owed you a living? No sane parent would say that, yet time and again, owners make this demand of their business.

Here's the truth: You owe everything to your business— all your time, effort, energy, and money. If it helps your business, you owe yourself the smallest salary you can take.

Along those same lines, ditch this idea that you've put your "blood, sweat, and tears" into your business. Owners love to use this line to justify the idea that their company owes them, but these words are nothing more than nonsense. When an owner says that, my reply is, "Show me on your last P&L report where you put blood, sweat, and tears."

The first step in reducing your cost to the company is

making sure you have the right mindset. Once you do, following these other steps is much easier.

YOUR TAX LIABILITY IS NOT YOUR TOP PRIORITY

It's not always an owner's fault if they're the biggest expense within their company. A lot of times, when I take over a struggling business, the previous owner was trying to do right by the company. Their efforts were simply misguided.

One common mistake owners make in growing companies is spending money primarily to reduce the company's tax liability. I've seen owners borrow $50,000 to buy a company car just for the $10,000 depreciation. Unless you're paying cash, exchanging tax liability for debt is not a smart business practice. Even with cash, it pays to be prudent.

If you take on debt to lessen your tax liability, what happens next year if things slow down, and you're still making payments? I'll tell you—the business loses money.

I took over a company once that had just bought a new twin engine plane. The bank was breathing down my neck and demanding fast results because they stood to lose a ton of money if the business went under. When I tried to sell the plane, I learned the difference in what the company owed on the plane and what it would bring was $150,000. I needed to eliminate this source of debt, but I didn't have $150,000 in the bank to pay it off.

I leased the plane to recover a portion of the monthly payment, but that purchase haunted us for years, despite the good intentions of the previous owner.

Like many owners, he fell into the trap of focusing on the wrong objective.

Tax liability is an important part of profitability, but you shouldn't seek to lower that number if doing so raises your expenses unnecessarily. If you truly need new equipment, the return on investment (ROI) numbers work in your favor, and the company can benefit from the tax write-off, make that purchase. If you're buying something for the tax benefits, you'll regret that decision very soon.

When you focus on the right objective, profitability, your tax liability becomes a secondary concern. If you must take a hit, better it be a bike (taxes) than a bulldozer (debt).

INCREASED EFFICIENCY HELPS REDUCE EXPENSES

When you talk about reducing expenses, most people's

minds jump to buying less of this or finding a better price on that. While important, saving money through reduced spending only takes you so far.

Eventually with cost cutting, you're going to hit a place where your reductions negatively impact the core business and degrade the customer experience. Before you go too far with cost cutting, look to reduce your expenses by improving your efficiency. In our companies, a significant chunk of our savings came from being more efficient.

One example comes from the manufacturing plant I mentioned back in Chapter One, the one that had been open seven years and never made a profit when I took over. In our first meeting, all we did was brainstorm ways to make our operation run smoother and quicker. Employees from every department gave input and nobody got upset over the suggested changes. We took the entire day coming up with new ideas.

The next day we shut the plant down and brought in tow motors to move equipment around based on employee feedback. Within thirty days of making these changes, we doubled production. As time went by, our efficiency continued to improve.

Part of the reason this company had never made a profit

was because it couldn't fill orders fast enough. By increasing efficiency, we had no problem keeping up with order demand. Not only that, we cut our overhead and labor costs in half for each product we made.

I can't think of a better example for everything we've covered in this book. I brought the team into the process, we created a plan, laid out some metrics, and took actions that reduced our expenses. The formula we followed is not rocket science. It's easy to replicate in any kind of business, because we all strive to do our jobs efficiently.

If your operation has areas that need improvement, don't sit around and complain. Call a company-wide meeting and brainstorm ideas to unclog the drain. I can promise you the men and women down in the trenches know how to get things moving again.

What I like most about increasing efficiency before reducing expenses is that, by perfecting the first one, you won't have to do as much work on the second.

OWNERS MUST COMMUNICATE WITH VENDORS

Building a solid relationship with your vendors is a huge part of expense control, which is why it's a mistake to exclusively rely on your team members to communicate with vendors. You should be the one on the phone, taking vendors out to lunch, visiting their businesses, and inviting them to see your operation. I've been in some high-tech companies, where I couldn't pronounce half the components we were ordering, but I still made those calls, because I know the value of building rapport with my vendors.

If you're looking for a local vendor, start by visiting their business, so you can explain what you do. To them, you represent profit, so they'll take the time to listen if you ask. Share your ninety-day plan with them and show where they fit into it. By doing so, you'll build trust and show the vendor your business is well organized.

Once you've built that relationship with a vendor, you can discuss better terms without the vendor hanging up the phone. Here's an example of how relationships with vendors can save you money.

Remember the purchase manager from Chapter One who bought $300,000 worth of steel without approval? When that happened, I was brand new to the company, but I figured I could leverage their existing relationship with the steel company to get terms that better suited our needs. I told the purchase manager to cancel the order he just placed, while I called the general manager of the steel company. Once I had him on the phone, I simply explained our situation:

- We typically ordered $300,000 worth of steel at a time.
- We only used $50,000 worth of steel a week.
- If the company kept an inventory, could we order the steel as needed?
- Would they consider moving us from thirty-day terms to sixty day?

The general manager couldn't have been more hospitable. He moved us to as-needed shipments that arrived within twenty-four hours and saved us from keeping inventory on-site. He also gave us forty-five-day terms and agreed to review sixty-day terms soon.

With one phone call, we picked up two weeks on paying and added $250,000 to our cash flow.

Building vendor relationships is not just good business, it's good for business. When a vendor knows your name and what your business does, they're going to work with you however and whenever they can. As an owner, you must hold up your end of the bargain by ensuring that relationship is profitable and enjoyable for the vendor, too.

When you go to re-bid vendor services each year, your

existing vendors will fight hard to give you the best pricing and terms, because they don't want to lose your business.

Another benefit of building those relationships is good vendors are a selling point for customers. If customers know your vendors are reliable and do good, timely work, it can help close deals, thereby adding tremendous value to your business.

Like anything worthwhile, those relationships take time to cultivate and work best when it's the owner making the effort. So, are there any vendors you need to call today?

SAVE MONEY WITH LARGE VENDORS AND INDEPENDENT CONTRACTORS

On large purchases (like $50,000 worth of steel per week), I've found you're better off going with large national vendors. Unlike mom-and-pop operations, large companies are more able to work with you on better terms or pricing. Small organizations usually need payment right away and can't afford to carry you on their accounts receivable.

If your purchases are small, I encourage you to use local vendors. If they're large, you need to build a relationship with the manager of the large vendor in your area.

Whenever you need plumbing, electrical, yard work,

painting, or other services, you can potentially save money by using independent contractors. There are benefits to working with large companies for these services, but their high overhead costs make them more expensive to employ. If you can find a licensed contractor who is reliable (not all of them are), they're going to be easier to work with and cheaper overall.

We've found, over the years, we save 30-50% annually using independent contractors. At the end of the year, we must pay workman's comp for those contractors, but that cost is relatively small compared to the savings we enjoy.

As with vendors, build relationships with your contractors and create a list of the ones you can count on to do good work, on time, and for a fair price.

LOOK FOR WAYS TO SAVE WITH EVERY PURCHASE

One thing to understand about expense reduction is when you begin, you're not going to find one egregious line item that fixes all your problems. Effective expense reduction is the accumulation of several little cuts. Here are some ideas:

⊘ Some vendors offer a 2–3% discount if you pay in ten days.

- If you'll use what you order, bulk pricing saves money.
- Turning off a computer when it's not in use has saved us up to $50 a year.
- We found big utility savings by switching to Nest thermostats.
- If the value of your property has gone up, leverage that loan-to-value ratio to refinance your mortgage and pay off short-term debt, especially any notes with high interest rates.
- Shop your credit card processing services to find better deals.
- Explore savings with insurance if you agree to a higher deductible.
- Don't hire full-time employees for jobs that can be outsourced.

At one point in our operating companies, we had seven full-time bookkeepers. Now, we use an outside bookkeeping firm to handle payroll, file state and federal reports, and compile our monthly P&Ls much cheaper than we were previously paying.

One simple way to reduce expense is to be organized. My mother was fond of saying "a place for everything and everything in its place." When employees are wandering around looking for something because it's misplaced, that's an example of costly disorganization.

Another way to cut costs is for your employees to stop stealing from you.

"Bob, what are you talking about?" you ask. "My employees don't steal from me!"

If you pay employees by the hour and they make two or three personal calls on the clock every day, they're stealing from you. Same story if they take extra-long lunch breaks or use office equipment, office supplies, or postage machines for personal business.

I don't browbeat my team with this rule. I just want them to remember we are there to benefit the company, not ourselves. If someone making $15 an hour spends twenty minutes a day on personal calls or goofing off, and the company works twenty days a month, that employee is costing the company $100 a month. It's not a huge deal with one employee, but if you have fifty employees doing the same, that's $60,000 a year in lost productivity. I want our team to think!

It might seem old school, but there are no sacred cows with expense reduction and control. You must turn over every rock and look for ways to improve your costs.

CONSIDER COSTS NOW AND DOWN THE ROAD

Has your business ever faced a manpower or equipment shortfall when it comes to filling a massive order on time? In those situations, did employees rationally seek out solutions, or did they run around with their ass on fire asking for new hires and new equipment?

I'm guessing it was the latter.

Educating employees on the art of purchasing, ROI, and the use of subcontractors can't start when crap hits the proverbial fan. When employees are stressed, they don't want to hear about expense control; they want the panic to subside. Before the big order arrives, explore the pros and cons of multiple options with your team.

Ask them what you'll do with new equipment and employees once the big order is filled. Is the company busy enough we can carry that new expense going forward?

Instead of making a rash decision to throw big money at this one order, can we rent, lease, or borrow the equipment we need? Can we outsource part of the work to a company with the capacity to help us fill the order? Put all your options out on the table.

When considering ROI, look at when that return will kick

in, and if it justifies the investment. If you need to purchase a $250,000 CNC machine and the payback time is five years, consider if you'll have enough work to utilize that machine consistently. If the answer is no, look at leasing it, even if the monthly lease payments exceed what you'd pay monthly on a purchase. You must weigh the short-term and long-term costs.

An alternative to outsourcing the work or hiring subcontractors is cross-training employees so they can help in other departments when needed. During my initial meetings with team members in a new company, I ask them to make a list of other departments they'd like to learn more about and help should the need arise. When slow times arise, I arrange with the managers of each department to train those folks who are interested.

Cross-training requires coordination and takes time, but there's no better way to deal with bottlenecks than by leveraging the skills of people who are already on the payroll.

The willingness of employees to learn new skills has never been an issue. Not only does cross-training give them insurance against being laid off during slow times, but it taps into their innate pride and their desire to do good work. You can call it naive, but once you teach your people about profitability and involving them in the process, you're going to see them pull together and learn new skills to help the business.

Another consideration is to pay employees overtime until the order is filled. Time and a half is expensive, but it beats the hell out of hoping new people you bring in can do the work. The people on your payroll have proven they know what they're doing, so wouldn't you rather pay them more and have assurance the job will get done right? If the increased workload stays consistent, then you can feel confident hiring new people.

You don't have to decide by yourself. State the obvious—that bringing on new employees will reduce everyone's bonuses—and let your team weigh the options.

GO TO YOUR BANK BEFORE YOU NEED MONEY

When it comes to banks, your first responsibility as the owner is to work with more than one. I hope the story from my early career—when my banker turned business partner died of a heart attack unexpectedly, leaving me with huge loans in my name—taught you the importance of having multiple bankers. It's like the Mack Truck Theory in reverse.

Like vendors, it's crucial to develop relationships with

your bankers before you ask them for money. Once the person in charge of your account knows and trusts you, your second responsibility is to educate them on what your business does, how it's going to grow, and your plan to get there. Invite them to your business to see it firsthand.

You never want to assume your banker knows everything they should about your business. I made that mistake years ago, when my business partner and I were working on the largest development we'd ever built. We invited our banker—a sharp young lady we'd worked with for years—to our office and spent the day going over our plan and the financials for our project so she could present our request to the loan committee.

When she left, we felt she had a good understanding of our project, so I was surprised to receive a call from her secretary a few days later asking me to come review our plans with her again. As I entered her office, I jokingly asked her, "Jan, are you getting senile in your old age? We just went over this a few days ago."

She wheeled around, eyes blazing, and said "Bethel, if you want a loan, sit your ass down and run through this, so I can sell it to the committee. I'm presenting requests for a new hospital, a mall, and a new automobile dealership, among others. Your job is to make sure I understand everything about your deal."

I was speechless, because I thought our deal was a "big deal."

Her outburst was a turning point that helped me fully grasp the difficulty of a banker's job. Customers march into a loan officer's office expecting them to know all about their business, which is an unfair and unrealistic expectation. In a day's time, a banker could talk to people in twenty or more industries. I left her office, realizing it was my job to educate my bankers about our business and our industry at large.

Over the years, I've also realized the importance of working with competent bankers. As my father used to say, "Be very careful around young horses and dumb bankers—both will run over you when you least expect it." I've been run over by both in my day, but thanks to Monticello Banking Company and their President and CEO Kenny Ramsey, I've only had to worry about young horses over the past decade.

Kenny is the sharpest banker I've ever worked with, and his team is equally as impressive—quick to respond, smart workers, understands the parts of a deal, and works well together. Everyone needs to do business with a bank like Monticello.

One day, we were in Kenny's office, and he shared some wisdom that applies to all business owners, not just bankers. "I'm tired of spending time with problem customers," he said. "I should be spending all my time with our good customers."

I took from his words this lesson: We shouldn't focus on the problems in our business and forget the customers who are loyal, pay on time, and cause no problems.

That's the beauty of educating your banker—they educate you as well.

The education process should always include a site visit. I've learned my team enjoys when bankers visit our business, and the bankers enjoy it, too. During those visits, team members take the banker through each department and explain how it fits into the larger view of the business. Because our employees took time to learn what each department does, everyone knows how they fit into the puzzle.

Before the banker arrives, we'll have a "dress rehearsal" of sorts. I don't have to train my people on how to speak intelligently about their department, but I want to make sure we're all bringing up the profitability tools we've worked hard to create:

- 🔗 "Let me show you where our department fits in the 90-day plan."
- 🔗 "Have you seen our daily operating control charts?"
- 🔗 "Here are some ways we've worked to reduce our expenses."

Bankers come away from their visits with a warm, fuzzy feeling and the assurance that we collectively know how the business operates. It's not all about the owner.

When you educate your loan officers, they can speak intelligently if a boss or an auditor asks for information about your business. Just because you send your bankers a copy of your monthly P&L report, doesn't mean they know what's going on within your business. It's your job as the owner to help them develop that understanding.

DON'T GET YOUR EQUITY TRAPPED BY THE BANK

Even when you're controlling expenses, you'll eventually need to bring new money into the company via the banks. When that time comes, your relationships can help you avoid a pitfall that snags many companies—having your equity trapped by the bank.

Here's what I mean by that. Say you're asking the bank for a $100,000 loan. As collateral, you're offering an unencumbered piece of equipment worth the same amount. If you've built a strong relationship with the banks, and they trust you and your business, they might loan you 80% of the value of that equipment, or $80,000.

If you haven't taken the time to develop relationships, bankers will usually default to what they're taught and minimize risk to the bank. So, instead of an 80% loan, they might offer you just 65% instead. With zero leverage, 65% is likely the best you can do.

When you take that loan, 35% of the value of that collateral is now trapped equity. You can't go to another bank and ask for a second loan on the remaining $35,000 value.

The only thing equity is good for is filling a row on your balance sheet.

The best way to guard against this is to work with banks long before you need a loan. If you nurture those relationships, you might still run into this situation, but at least you'll have other options to explore. You're not trapped with just one way forward.

THE RELATIONSHIP BETWEEN TIME, QUALITY, AND PRICE

Your interactions with customers hold one final key to expense control. To avoid losing money on each sale, you should allow customers to choose two of the following three factors: Time, quality, and price. Whatever two they pick, you get the third one:

- If a customer wants a high-quality product in a hurry, the price will be high.
- If a customer wants a cheap product done quickly, the quality will be low.
- If a customer wants a high-quality product for cheap, it's going to take time.

Most companies pride themselves on quality and throw that variable out of the mix, leaving just time and price. Do customers want it done cheap or want it done quick?

If you let the customer dictate both, or all three, you're putting yourself in a bad position. You're either going to lose money, or your production team is going to hate you.

When you can master the relationship between these

three factors, and add that to the other changes we've talked about, your business will be lean, efficient, and profitable. If you're starting where my seventy-seven businesses started from, that's a huge accomplishment.

You should be very proud of the work you've done to turn around your business or forestall any future struggles, but the journey isn't quite over yet. There's still one variable to this equation and it's the most important one for sustained success:

You must lead your business as well as manage it. Let's look at how that happens.

6

THINK AND ACT LIKE A LEADER

When I step into a business as the new owner, I do so as an outsider with a narrow view of how the business operates. Therefore, it is to my benefit to keep the previous owner or CEO around in some capacity, so I can leverage their knowledge and expertise to aid in our turnaround. I've tried to do that in every business I've taken over for the banks.

Without fail, I've had to let each owner go in a short period.

Rather than making my life easier by speeding up our recovery, previous owners tended to hinder our progress with their poisonous "my way or the highway" behavior. Whenever they staunchly defended their poor financial decisions—such as a massive expense account, company cars, and a private jet—I saw in them the drunk businessman who was handsome, smart, rich, bulletproof, and radiation proof.

Any new ideas from me or the employees were met with skepticism or outright rejection. I should've trademarked the phrase "that won't work" based on how often I heard it from previous owners. Call me a naive fool, but I went into each new business with the hope *this time* would be different from all the others.

Much to my disappointment, each attempt inevitably ended with dismissal.

Based on that statement, you might think I have a low opinion of business owners. Nothing could be further from the truth. I've been a business owner for more than fifty years, so I know the courage it takes to step out in faith and risk everything you have to start or buy a business.

I've dedicated my career to helping small and medium-sized businesses, because I believe they are the lifeblood of every country's economy, not just the United States. I wrote this book to help business owners with the skills they need for sustained business success. When owners adopt the right mindset and the right approach, businesses flourish.

The challenge is none of us are born with the skills needed to lead a business.

If you're an engineer who decides to start a business around a product you've created, you will cease being an engineer on day one in your new company. The list of your job duties will grow exponentially, and none of them will include building your product.

David Packard, who co-founded Hewlett-Packard (HP) with Bill Hewlett, realized early on his engineering background hadn't prepared him to lead a business. When he and Hewlett started their company in that tiny garage in Palo Alto, Packard did not go in with the mindset of "I'm the CEO." Instead, he played to his strengths and learned over time what it meant to be not just an operating officer at HP but also a leader.

His story demonstrates the importance of being intentional in developing your leadership skills and learning parts of your business that fall outside your areas of strength. Packard didn't try to do every job himself, but he knew what those jobs entailed. Any role that didn't utilize his talents was delegated to someone more capable and available than him.

At the same time, he and Hewlett never lost sight of their responsibility to be leaders in their business, the technology community, and the world at large.

BUSINESS OWNERS MUST LEAD, NOT MANAGE PEOPLE

When asked about the role of owners within their business, T. Boone Pickens, one of my business heroes, quoted Grace Hopper, the best-known female admiral in the U.S. Navy: "She expressed my management philosophy succinctly when she said, 'You don't manage people, you manage things. You lead people.' She was right."

Pickens and Hopper said it better than I ever could, and their words apply to the owners of every business large or small and regardless of industry.

If you're not leading your business, who is?

History remembers Franklin D. Roosevelt, Winston Churchill, Margaret Thatcher, and other luminaries as leaders, not managers. They managed armies, countries, and wars, but we remember them most for their ability to inspire hope and empower their people.

The job of a business owner is no different. Your employees are looking at you to not only sign their paychecks, but to lead them through times both good and bad. Leadership is one role you can't delegate to someone else. When you're the one making decisions, the entire staff will take its cues from you on how to react to any given situation.

Much like business ownership, we aren't born being natural leaders. We learn how to lead through observation and relentless study of successful leaders throughout history. I've read every article and book I can find written about great leaders from history and successful business leaders like T. Boone Pickens, Jack Welch, Bill Gates, and Warren Buffett. I learn so much from studying their methods and seeing how they responded to success and failure.

I encourage you to find leaders you admire and read about them. The more you research their leadership, the more you can apply the lessons they've learned.

The role of leadership in today's workplace is much different from what I saw growing up in a post-World War II world. That era was defined by hard-ass owners who could treat their employees like crap, because fifty more people were waiting for jobs if anyone quit. Today's owners are expected to lead responsibly and teach others how to lead, as well.

When you hire good people, both jobs are easy. Responsible employees don't need to be managed; they just need to be pointed in the right direction and turned loose. You can empower your team to do their jobs at the highest possible level by giving them the tools they need, be it new equipment, additional staff, or professional development.

When you raise up new leaders within your business, make sure to give them the authority they need to do their jobs. Remember from Chapter Three that owners must respect the org chart and avoid going behind their managers' backs to get things done. You should also avoid reprimanding managers in front of their teams. Address problems in your office to maintain the authority you've given your company's leaders.

The best way to impart these lessons on others is to lead by example.

GOOD LEADERS ARE OPTIMISTIC AND LEVEL-HEADED

When I take over a new business, I personally guarantee the debt owed by that company, which means if we fail, I'm on the hook for that money. With that much skin in the game, the only behavior I can afford to bring to work is relentless optimism. No matter how your company is doing, your first step to leading by example is being optimistic.

Anybody can be a pessimist, but it takes guts to be an optimist.

There have been plenty of days I wanted to curl up in the fetal position on the floor of my office and feel sorry for myself. Since I didn't have the money to afford failure, I didn't have time for those outbursts of pessimism or negative thinking.

When you own a business, you lose the right to bring your emotions to work every morning. You don't get to be pissed off one day because you got in a fight with your wife, then be sunshine and rainbows the next day. If you can't check your negative emotions at the door every morning, your leadership will suffer dramatically.

Your employees are counting on you for consistent leadership. They need to see the same leader every day, one who brings a positive attitude, calm demeanor, and business-like approach to work. If you're angry or down in the dumps, you can't listen effectively, offer encouragement, or help solve the problems that reach your desk.

You can't be an effective leader when your behavior isn't right.

Within my companies, I tell managers if their personal problems will inhibit them from having an optimistic attitude at work, they should stay home and deal with those issues. Although I'm available to talk, I don't need an explanation. All they must do is call and tell me they won't be in that day. I'd rather they take a day or two and clear their heads than bring negativity into the workplace and drag everyone else down.

If you worry employees would abuse this privilege, my experience says you've no need for concern. I've made this offer to hundreds of mangers over fifty-two years and had about fifteen days someone stayed home. I see those missed days as an investment in the mental welfare of the team and the positive workplace cultures we built.

Good behavior also demands being calm in the face of bad news. When I was young, my dad would jump down my throat for all sorts of silly mistakes I made. When terrible things happened, like me totaling four new cars within a one-year period, he was as calm as if we were sitting by the lake fishing. Each time I called him, he asked if anyone was hurt and said he'd be there right away. He didn't raise his voice or chastise me.

In those stressful situations, I needed my dad's reassuring

demeanor. Business leaders should adopt the same response to crisis. Your employees will hide things from you if they know you'll raise a million dollars' worth of hell at their mistakes. Temper tantrums from owners lead to employee secrets, and secrets can lead to big trouble down the road.

When employees bring you bad news, take a deep breath and ask yourself, "What's the worst that could come out of this mistake? If that worst-case scenario comes true, will it still be a big deal a year from now?" The emotional part of our brain likes to make mountains out of molehills, but if we'll stop and apply logic, we'll find there are few things worth getting upset over. The few that are worth it should still be handled with grace.

As the leader, if you panic or fly off the handle, everyone else will follow suit.

SEEK OUT THE HELP YOU NEED

I once took over a company so far under water, the lead bank's special asset department gave me thirty days to see what we could do before I had to assume the company's debt, which was several million dollars and in default. In addition, the accounts payable were over $900,000 and most were ninety days past due.

At first, there did not appear to be enough money on earth to save this company. However, the company's customers were worldwide, and as I looked at the contracts they were working on, I saw hope.

The banks told me, in addition to assuming the debt of the company, I had to put $1 million in escrow to assure the continued operation of the business. This was insurance to the lenders that I would not sell the assets to fund operations. It seemed to be a hurdle too high to jump.

On day one, I called a company-wide meeting and gave the team the details, including the fact I had thirty days to decide if we could make it work. I told the team we had to develop a ninety-day plan in twenty-four hours because I was going to call on some of our customers to see if they would help. There were several customers the company had multimillion-dollar contracts with, and I hoped we could use this to our advantage.

While the team went to work on the plan, I contacted the head of a division of ENI, the Italian oil and gas giant. I told him I needed to meet with him urgently, and he told me to come to Milan. I left on the next plane, but before I left, I also called on another giant company in France, the nuclear group Framatome, and one in Saudi Arabia,

Saudi Aramco, all of which had very large contracts with the company.

I took our plan with me, a list of bankers I had worked with in other turnarounds, and my thirty-day contract with the lead bank.

After an all-night flight, I walked into the office of the managing director of one of ENI's companies, a man I'd never met. I explained exactly the status of the company, handed him the plan and list of bankers, took a deep breath, and said, "I need you to advance us a million dollars against your contract to save this company."

I knew his division badly needed the work we were doing, but was it worth the gamble of a million dollars to a broke company?

He stared at me for what seemed an hour, picked up our plan, glanced at the list of bankers, and said, "What are the odds you can pull this off?"

I told him if he would give us the advance, 100%.

Again, he stared at me a couple of minutes and said, "Do you have wiring instructions for your bank?" I handed him the instructions, he picked up his phone, gave someone instructions in Italian, stuck out his hand, and said, "It's done. Now, go back and finish our job." I was so weak; I could hardly walk out of his office.

Boy, he had guts, and boy, was that power, I thought.

We worked for ENI for the next seven years, he and I became great friends, and everyone on our team never forgot what he had done for us. When we got a call from ENI, no one griped about jumping on the next plane anywhere on earth they needed us.

Next, I jumped on a plane to Paris, where I got another advance from a large customer, Framatome, and then headed to Saudi Arabia where I got the third advance. The trip had lasted three days, and I felt we could save the company, so when I got back, I went to the bank and signed the papers to assume the company's debt.

My next task was to keep the company's creditors from throwing us into bankruptcy. I had our accounting department create a list with the largest payable descending to the smallest.

I called the head of each company and went to see them. I took our plan, the list of bankers, and a copy of each international wire transfer. I told each creditor our plan was to use cash flow to fund operations and every dime above that would go to our accounts payable, pro rata. For example, if their payable represented 10% of total payables, and we had excess cash flow of $10,000, they would get $1,000. To unsecured creditors, this is a much better deal than five cents on the dollar in bankruptcy court.

It was not a hard sale, because the company had lied to these folks and not returned their calls, so when someone showed up and took responsibility, they were willing to work something out. I asked each person to sign beside their company's name so I could use it for leverage with others.

I was on a roll until I walked into an advertising company we owed $55,000.

The owner sat red-faced behind the desk as I walked in, and before I could introduce myself, he barked, "Did you bring my money?" I told him I hadn't, and he responded by threatening to throw our company into bankruptcy and asking me to leave.

I left and came back the next day. He let me get a few minutes into explaining my plan, before asking me to leave once more. On the third and fourth day, he refused to talk with me. On day five, I met him in the parking lot and pleaded for five minutes of his time.

"You're the most determined SOB I've ever seen," he told me. "Come on in."

I left with his signature on my list.

Not only that, but within a few weeks, this man who wouldn't give me the time of day became part of our team. He attended one of our company-wide meetings, where he got to see our DOC boards and heard from each employee their role within our plan. After that meeting, he increased the money we owed him to help us.

When we paid him off a year later, I made sure to include a bonus on his check as our way of saying "thank you" for assisting with our company's turnaround. As I walked into his office to present the check, tears came to this man's eyes.

"I've never enjoyed anything like working with that team for the past year," he told me.

He remained our advertising agency for the next seven years, until we sold the company to a large, public company in Houston. In those seven years, we made incredible profit and became well-known within our industry. As I reflect on our success, and how it began from such despair, I'm reminded of this verse from Matthew 7:7: "Ask and it will be given to you, seek and you will find, knock and the door will be opened to you."

All we did was ask for help...and it worked!

As a business owner, it's easy to succumb to pride and believe you must fix it all yourself. That's not the case. If you have faith in your team, work smart, implement your plan, and track your results, you can find the help you need if you seek it out.

In the words of my father, when you seek help, "Be bold in everything you do."

YOU SHOULD ALWAYS BE THE LAST TO LEAVE

Within most of my companies, there are more jobs I can't do than jobs I can do. I can help with purchasing, reporting, and accounting, but I can't weld, solder, test equipment, or perform millions of other jobs. However, one way I can always help my team is by being the first to arrive and the last to leave every day to support them. To me, this is required of good leaders.

We've pulled all-nighters in my companies before to get a project finished and delivered on time. I would have been useless down in the trenches, but I made coffee, picked up dinner, and grabbed supplies from the stockroom to show my team support.

During the week, I like to work with my office door open, so the employees know I'm there to help them how ever I can.

As the boss, you have every right to roll in at 9 am and leave at 3 pm for a trip to the country club. However, what kind of example are you setting for your team?

In one of my companies, we had a young electrical engineer with massive potential. He had undergraduate and graduate degrees in electrical engineering from a great university, plus he was quick, sharp, and creative. He was one of those employees you built a team around, so we quickly made him a department head.

We had just pulled this company out of the ditch and sat on the precipice of several big international jobs that would add huge profit to our company over the next few years. I knew our prized engineer would be crucial to the success of these jobs, so I decided to incentivize his performance by offering him 5% stock in the company for free.

Judging by his reaction, it seemed he understood his new-found responsibilities as a well-compensated team leader and a newly minted company stockholder.

Just a couple days later, I realized, much to my horror, that my plan had backfired.

It was 5 pm on a day when I knew we'd all be there late into the evening. I was in the break room pouring coffee when I heard someone ask the engineer, "Are you leaving?"

His response caused me to spill coffee everywhere.

"Benefit of ownership," he replied with unbearable smugness.

With that, I dashed out of the break room and pulled him into my office for a meeting where it took every ounce of strength for me to maintain my composure.

"You can forget the stock," I told him. "You proved to me in two days you're not worthy of it. Go ahead and leave, but understand you and I are back to ground zero, and I'm extremely disappointed in how you handled this situation."

In that moment, our engineer had allowed his ego to overwhelm his judgment.

His behavior changed quickly after our meeting. He worked hard to redeem himself and earn back my trust over the next few years, but that only happened after I firmly reminded him of the expectations we had for all team members.

Had I not modeled the behavior I expected of my engineer, I'd have walked into that meeting as nothing more than a hypocrite spouting empty words.

If you're going to preach it, you must practice it. Otherwise, you're going to come up short in those moments where your leadership is most needed.

CONSIDER HOW YOU COMMUNICATE

From what I've found, the communication within successful organizations shares two common characteristics: clarity and optimism. Knowing that, there are certain words and phrases I recommend you remove from you and your team's vocabulary.

Fail words like "can't," "but," "fault," and "blame" don't belong in successful organizations. Growing up, my mother would tell us, "Tell me you will or won't do something, but don't tell me you can't!" She also liked to say "but" is something you sit on, not a word you use in conversation, so I grew to despise "can't" and "but" early in life.

I have no interest in words like "fault" and "blame,"

because I'd rather fix the problem, not point fingers. Time is money, and I don't want to waste either assigning blame.

These fail words—can't, but, fault, blame, and more—negatively affect your team's psyche, cause backbiting, lower morale, and lead to lackluster performance. Optimistic leaders shouldn't use them and neither should your team. Toss these words out!

Another word I've thrown out is "if." With headlight accounting, we deal with what's in front of us, not a theoretical "if." When our team sets a goal, I want them saying, "When we meet this goal," not "If we meet this goal." Do you see the difference? While not an outright fail word, "if" gives you an escape hatch for when the going gets tough. When you're safeguarding your business against failure, using the escape hatch isn't an option.

I suggest reading the poem "If" by Rudyard Kipling if you're interested in "if."

I know it's an age thing, but a pet peeve of mine is when people say, "No problem," rather than, "You're welcome," whenever I thank them. Again, that's a personal thing, but I do appreciate when someone says, "You're welcome." I find it more respectful.

Another expression that drives me crazy is ASAP. This word is completely useless, yet we hear it all the time in the corporate world. If someone asks me to meet them ASAP, I can't look at my watch or calendar and know when that is, so why would they ever say it?

Depending on the intent of the person who says it and the person who hears it, ASAP can mean five minutes or five days. When you or your team members ask for something, make sure to specify a time frame. If it's ten minutes, communicate that and see if the other party can oblige. Saying "ASAP" causes confusion and wastes time.

While your words are important, how you communicate also sends a strong message. I made the mistake early in my career of not being honest with my employees when they messed up. Rather than shooting them straight, I softened the blow and beat around the bush to avoid hurting their feelings. All that got me was repeated mistakes and further frustration.

I learned that employees value straightforward and supportive feedback. You can set them back on track without being an ass about it. Be clear and concise in your feedback and make sure employees understand what you've told them. The last thing you want is for someone to leave a meeting with you saying, "What the hell was he talking about?"

If you'll avoid fail words and nonsense corporate jargon, plus shoot it straight with your employees, the lines of communication in your company will be firing on all cylinders.

BEING A BLANK SLATE CAN BE ADVANTAGEOUS

I've learned many invaluable lessons in my career working alongside some of the most successful businessmen in Tennessee, including this idea of being a blank slate to your employees in terms of religious and political beliefs.

For some owners, being closed off might be the exact opposite of their approach. I would never suggest all leaders *must* be blank slates, but I'd like to point out a few of the reasons I see value in keeping my private life private when I'm at work.

First, I've been blessed to work with people of all different religions and nationalities, and I've realized when you strip away the labels we attach to people, we all have the same desires for our lives—happiness, security, and fulfillment, among others. After working with so many different people and realizing this truth, I've developed a disinterest in other people's religion and politics.

I don't care who you voted for or where you go to church, if in fact you do. The same logic applies in reverse: Nobody should care about my politics or religion. The outcome I've seen most often when owners are outspoken on these issues is they alienate people within their company who feel differently. I don't want to make others feel like outsiders due to their beliefs.

We also live in a hyper-sensitive world that is easily offended. Revealing your political affiliations is all some people need to turn on you. When that happens, and all they can think about when you're around is, "Shut up, you stinkin' Republican/Democrat," you're going to have a hard time getting through to them ever again.

I also shy away from revealing too much about my family life. This goes back to checking my emotions at the door each morning, but I also don't want employees using personal information I share to try to gain brownie points.

I try with my team to know the names of their spouses and children and ask about them, but I don't crack the door much wider than that. I will support my team when a personal issue is affecting their performance, but ultimately, my job title is owner, not therapist.

Furthermore, I think the issue of employee attitude is overblown.

I'm more interested in employee behavior than attitude. If you have a bad attitude, but it doesn't affect your performance, I don't care. If your attitude influences your behavior to the detriment of the company, then we've got a problem.

Plenty of management books focus on improving employees' attitudes, but I see it as a waste of time. What I'm interested in is behavior and performance. Teammates and opponents would say Michael Jordan's attitude was terrible, especially when he lost. I see a guy who won six rings and is considered the best basketball player of all time. His performance was what mattered, not his attitude.

THE TWO RULES EVERY COMPANY SHOULD ESTABLISH

With a focus on behavior, there are two rules I implement in new businesses:

1. I will not curse at you, nor will I be cursed at by anyone.
2. There's always room for discussion, but there's no room for ugliness.

If I reprimand employees, I do so privately without raising

my voice or cursing at them. Whenever someone steps into my office to share their ideas, I expect the same courtesy. Refraining from shouting and profanity feeds into the respectful environment I expect within all my businesses, and I have zero tolerance for violations of this rule.

I've only had one employee test this policy. A gentleman lost his temper over a coworker doing something I'd asked that coworker to do, and he stormed into my office shouting and swearing at me. He left my office swearing with his final paycheck in hand.

These two rules apply to the entire team. We're not going to be insensitive or bully other people. In everything we do, we're going to show respect. Disagreements will still exist, but those differences are resolved with open, decent discussion. I don't expect everyone to be best friends, but I do expect team members to be able to work together.

I have zero tolerance for workplace tension, thanks to an experience early in my career.

In one of the first businesses I took over, the two women who worked in the office—one older and one younger—shared a strong dislike for each other. I hadn't been on the job long when the young woman came into my office teary-eyed and told me all the mean things the older woman had said and done. Being in my twenties, I hadn't figured out how to handle conflict quite yet, so I told her I'd talk to the older woman.

When I called the other woman into my office, I beat around the bush before finally telling her what the younger woman had said. Of course, this did nothing but cause the older woman to become defensive and degrade the younger woman. Not entirely interested in their problems, I asked them both to get along and assumed I'd solved the problem.

A handful of teary-eyed office visits later, I realized I'd solved nothing.

One morning, when I was overwhelmed by a heavy workload, the young woman came flying into my office with soggy cheeks. In the heat of frustration, I finally snapped. I called the older woman into my office and fired them both on the spot.

With that, I stormed out of my office, got in my car, and left the premises. I was red-faced and shaking all over. I'm sure my blood pressure was sky high. After driving around for thirty minutes to cool off, I came back to work and saw both their cars in the parking lot. I quickly went to my office and closed the door, so I wouldn't have to see them as they left.

Soon as I sat down, there was a tiny knock at my door. Both women walked in, puffy-eyed from crying, and asked if I'd give them another chance. Not wanting to do their jobs myself, I agreed. They worked for the company five more years and never uttered another ugly word about each other. In fact, they became great friends!

I'm not proud of how I handled that situation, but I'm glad I went through it. Dealing with conflict so early in my career showed me how workplace tension and animosity drags everyone down. As the leader, you must demand respect from everyone and maintain a zero-tolerance policy for ugliness, bullying, animosity, or tension.

If there's conflict, deal with it constructively. When it festers, you might snap one day and fire two valuable employees when their turmoil pushes you over the edge!

CLEAN DESKS LEAD TO INCREASED PRODUCTIVITY

I learned another valuable lesson early in my career, this time from a retired business partner: Business owners should be concerned with making money, not making a living.

You see, one of my first companies dealt with real estate, and I spent twelve hours a week filling out reports. In my mind, I was doing important work that fell under the owner's purview. A visit from my business partner showed me the error of my ways. When he walked in one morning and saw the stack of papers on my desk, he asked:

"Why are you handling that and not accounting?"

"Accounting doesn't know how to file these reports yet," I told him.

"Get all these reports off your desk," he replied. "Take a few hours and teach accounting how to file them, then take ten minutes each day to review their work. Your focus should be on the efficiency and profitability of the company, not paperwork."

His words angered me because, deep down, I knew he was right. I thought I was doing the work owners should do, but he made me realize I was wasting time with reports I should've handed off to someone else from the start.

My business partner thought like an owner, which meant he thought about making money. Before that moment, I thought like an employee who had a stack of paperwork to finish. His words inspired me to change my thinking and adopt an important rule:

Business owners should have clean desks and open eyes.

The amount of paperwork owners are responsible for is staggering. It's easy to get bogged down in repetitive tasks that should be pushed as far down the org chart as possible.

Department heads should adopt this philosophy, as well. I want the leaders in my companies thinking about profitability and efficiency along with me, not sitting behind a desk stacked high with papers that should be handed off to someone else.

When repetitive tasks are pushed down the org chart, it frees up valuable time leaders can use to focus on important issues. Your employees will also appreciate you entrusting them with more responsibility. Take time to train the parties responsible for these tasks and review their work to ensure it meets the company's standards.

Paperwork is not unimportant. It's simply an unnecessary burden for owners to carry.

If you want to improve your productivity, you should aim for every desk in your company to be clean. This is especially helpful in smaller companies, where each employee shares more of the responsibility for profitability and efficiency.

I learned this lesson in uncomfortable fashion at International Nuclear Inc., which was the first company I was involved in purchasing. The two gentlemen I worked with to purchase that business, John "Jack" DeWitt and Ray Weiland, were two of the most brilliant men I've ever met. Jack was a legend in the world of broadcast, having started WSM radio and WSM television in Nashville, which birthed the Grand Ole Opry.

International Nuclear was a research, design, development, and manufacturing company that employed a lot of engineers. On day one, after the purchase closed, Jack and Ray asked all the engineers to take personal items from their desks to their cars, which they did. Once that was finished, the duo emptied every desk and filing cabinet drawer of its contents.

They piled everything—drawings, pencils, envelopes, letterhead, staplers—onto carts and returned it to the stockroom. The engineers were understandably upset we were raiding their desks, and as a young guy, I was embarrassed, because I didn't understand why Jack and Ray were doing this on day one.

During a break, I turned to them and asked, "Why are we doing this?"

Together, they laid out three compelling reasons for their actions:

1. They wanted to be able to measure the work the engineers were doing, and they couldn't do that when their desks were covered with papers.
2. The engineers were keeping original drawings at their desks after they finished with them, causing other engineers to waste time searching for them.
3. We had enough office supplies to last for years, but nobody knew it, because all the supplies were shoved in filing cabinets or buried on people's desks.

My embarrassment turned to understanding as I, along with the engineers, understood the purpose behind clearing out the desks. Rather quickly, this company that had been going downhill generated a profit, because the work was measured, and the people were focused. As crazy as it sounds, clean desks sparked that transformation.

If the desks in your business, including yours, are stacked high with junk, clean them off. Hand off those tasks that don't require your time to someone else. Reorganizing your desk and your responsibilities can shift your mindset and transform your productivity.

THE DOCUMENTS THAT DRIVE DECISION MAKING

When you prioritize a clean desk, you discover the stack of papers needed to make decisions regarding profitability is quite small. On my desk, for instance, are one-page summaries from our CPA office analyzing our areas of cost.

As we know, costs are the part of the profitability equation we can control, yet so often owners neglect to monitor their costs, because it's not a pressing concern. Even if they do prioritize this task, where can they find time to compile the relevant data?

Here is yet another reason we hire an outside CPA office to help with accounting. When you can ask a third party to compile data from previous years in areas of costs ranging from raw materials to insurance, staying on top of expenses becomes manageable.

With their reports in hand, for example, I can see at a glance the cost to make my product increased 5% each of the past three years. To offset that 15% decrease in profits, we could increase our prices by 5% annually, or perhaps increase prices 15% every three years. Whatever route we choose, this knowledge empowers our decision making.

I mentioned earlier we own apartment complexes. During the recession, rental rates fell through the floor, so we decreased our prices along with our competitors. Once the recession ended, rental rates rose at a breakneck pace to all-time highs.

One of the documents I had on my desk during that time was a breakdown of how our competitors were raising their prices to capitalize on this increased demand. I saw increases ranging from 5–8%, so I raised our prices to match. Staying on top of market trends helped us avoid leaving money on the table.

So, as you push repetitive tasks down the org chart and clear time in your schedule, make sure to fill those new-found hours with consistent cost monitoring.

When you ask for data from your CPA office, the documents they send should be short and concise, thus ensuring well-informed decisions can be made quickly.

TAKE A HOLISTIC VIEW OF YOUR BUSINESS

One mistake I've seen countless owners make is caring only about the areas of their business that interest them. The engineer from earlier in this chapter who started his own company can't spend all his time in engineering. Even if he has no interest in accounting, sales, marketing, and human resources, he needs to learn about those departments, if he wants to be an effective leader in a successful business.

I had the advantage of a father who knew the value of being well-rounded and made me learn about every department at the car dealership starting at age fourteen.

For many owners, their strength is also their greatest weakness. The engineer is naturally drawn to engineering at the expense of other departments that are equally important to his success. Chefs would rather cook than crunch numbers in the accounting office, while mechanics wants to fix cars, not sort through payroll.

We all have areas of interest we gravitate toward, but as a business owner, you must understand the process of how every job in your company is done, even if you can't do it yourself. Without a proper understanding, you won't know what proficiency looks like in each role, nor will you be prepared to hire someone for those jobs.

You can hire the top accounting personnel available and puff out your chest over the top-notch team you've assembled. However, how do you know that's true? If you haven't learned what good accounting looks like, those new accountants you're proud to have hired could be terrible at their jobs, and you would never know.

If you're in a large company, you can hire a general manager to oversee and track the progress of each department. Until your company grows enough to warrant (and afford) that person, you have to fill the GM role yourself.

When I helped negotiate the purchase of International Nuclear, Jack and Ray brought me on as the general manager. I couldn't do the engineering work, but I learned how each job contributed to the whole, so I could measure the efficiency of each. In a company that large, there were reports that had to be filed I wasn't familiar with, so I had the accountant teach me the purpose and deadline for each.

Even if you hire a general manager, you must still serve as the conductor of your orchestra. Imagine a scenario where your daily operating controls show cash flow next month will be small. Meanwhile, your purchasing department has several large purchases lined up during that time frame. When you're focused on keeping your business in sync, you can address this problem, before it bites you.

All you must do is bring purchasing and accounting together, explain the cash flow situation, and ask purchasing to hold off on any non-essential purchases.

We learned in Chapter Three that out-of-control growth

can create weak links within a business that will snap at the most inopportune time. Weak links are also created when owners let certain departments slide through the cracks.

When one link breaks, the whole chain (your business) weakens.

You can't delegate your role as the conductor to someone else, not even the general manager. If you own the business, it is your duty to ensure all the moving parts are in sync and working as efficiently as possible.

GOOD LEADERSHIP CREATES COMPANY-WIDE ACCOUNTABILITY

It is your obligation as the leader of your business to be accountable to your team. It is your opportunity to shape yourself through mindful improvement into a great leader.

When you accept that opportunity, you'll create accountability within your business.

The first step is implementing headlight accounting. When everyone knows who is doing what to whom, when, and for how much, there's zero ambiguity. If production agrees to make 1,000 units a day as part of your thirty-day plan, accountability has been created within that department.

If they only produce 750, you know where to go to fix the problem.

Everyone in the company, including the leadership, must own their part of the process and be held accountable for their agreed-upon contribution. This explains why headlight accounting should involve your full team and produce attainable goals.

The second step is communicating clearly and frequently with your team. Weekly meetings will keep the lines of communication open, but it's up to you to avoid unclear directions. Remember ASAP is not a time frame and beating around the bush helps no one.

Your team can only feel accountable when they understand what you say and appreciate why you're saying it. Clarity and buy-in create alignment around a shared goal, whereas if you're vague and force-feed goals to your team, they're going to shut you down.

ALL PROBLEMS MUST COME WITH POSSIBLE SOLUTIONS

Does it ever feel like the problems that reach your desk are the big, ugly, scary ones that nobody knows how to solve? I remember one such moment early in my career when we were working on-site at the Virginia Electric

Power Company as a subcontractor for Westinghouse Electric Nuclear Division. I had never seen such a tightly planned operation.

I understood why, though: If the nuclear plant were to shut down for any reason, the cost of replacing that power from off the grid cost more than $500,000 per day.

So, imagine my horror when the number two manager came running up to me and the Westinghouse project manager, breathing heavily and with his metaphorical ass clearly on fire. His exact words escape me, but his message was, "We can't do what you're trying to do."

I'll never forget what happened next.

The Westinghouse manager got in the guy's face and told him, "There's no such word as 'can't.' Given enough money and time, I can put a man on the moon. I want you to come up with options, then tell me which of those options you want to try first."

Ever since that day, I've opted for the approach that manager took. Gone are the days when employees can roll a grenade into my office and say, "Here, fix this."

Now, whenever my team brings me a problem, that

problem must come with options for solving it. It doesn't matter how well I know the various departments within my business, the employees still know them better than I do. Therefore, it only makes sense they be the ones to generate options when problems arise.

One of the main reasons employees bring problems to the owner is they're up against some sort of time crunch. You can deal with this by reiterating during meetings problems should be brought to light right away, not two hours before a solution is needed. Problem-solving could be your professional super power, but nobody is capable of effectively solving problems when they're that far behind the 8-ball.

A sense of urgency on the part of your team must be met with a sense of understanding on your end. The options your employees suggest aren't always going to work. In fact, most of the time you'll be down to Plan C before the right answer emerges.

You should let employees know they're not going to be punished if their solutions don't work. The act of trying to solve the problem and failing is far better than ignoring the problem and hoping it goes away. If you raise hell every time a solution doesn't pan out, your employees will conceal issues rather than get their ass chewed.

When your team is generating possible solutions, leave room for even the wackiest ideas. You don't have to try every idea, but you should allow room for creativity during the brainstorming phase. If you squash ideas before they've had a chance to breathe, your best problem-solvers will keep their mouths shut to avoid being embarrassed.

Once all the options are on the table, make a list based on which ones are most likely to succeed and have your team work on the best option right away. Don't let team members get discouraged if none of the options on their list solve the problem.

Failure is only detrimental if you don't use the data provided to learn, grow, and try a different approach. If all options are exhausted, come back together as a team armed with the knowledge of what didn't work and create a fresh list of ideas.

I can't tell you when you'll find the solution, but I know tenacity and teamwork have conquered every problem our companies have faced the past five decades.

REACH OUT TO OTHER LEADERS IN YOUR INDUSTRY

When I first took over businesses, stepping into an industry where I had zero experience left me intimidated. What did I know about owning apartment complexes, running a restaurant, or leading an engineering company? As a general manager, I could learn how to price and measure the work, but there were still gaps I wanted to fill.

In addition to asking the staff tons of questions, I made a habit of picking up trade journals and doing online research to find the top leaders in my industry.

Once I identified those people, I simply picked up the phone and called the number one person on the list. I rarely reached them directly, so I'd leave a message with the secretary explaining who I was and ask for five minutes with their boss to ask for advice.

Based on this perception we have of successful business owners guarding their secrets and refusing to help competitors, you might think I got few, if any, callbacks.

In fifty-two years, I've had that call returned every single time.

When I got that person on the phone, I asked if I could come visit them for fifteen minutes and get some advice. Again, I've never had an owner turn down that request.

Here's a perfect example: After buying a company with

a division that produced robot components, I called Joe Engelberger, the president of Unimation, the world's first, and at one point, largest, manufacturer of industrial robots. Although his operation was in Connecticut, I asked if I could visit him and pick his brain for fifteen minutes, since I didn't know the first thing about robots. He happily agreed to meet with me.

I ended up spending two days with Joe receiving a Ph.D. level crash course in robotics. For the cost of a plane ticket, I got a better education than I could've received anywhere else. I left that visit with the confidence I needed to push our products into the marketplace.

Furthermore, Joe was a delight to be around. He walked me through his plant and took me out to dinner. I came for advice and ended up making a wonderful connection.

I've used this strategy time and again when I enter new industries, and I've been shocked by the willingness of people to help. Years ago, I read an article in *Fortune* magazine on two brothers from Houston who were the leading authorities in oil and gas consulting. I was reading that article because I'd just purchased a company that manufactured equipment for the oil and gas industry. The minute I finished the article, I picked up the phone to call the brothers and was surprised when I got through to them on the first attempt.

They agreed to meet with me for fifteen minutes, no questions asked. Our meeting ended up lasting half a day and was extremely helpful.

The help you need is out there if you'll just seek it out. This strategy works great, even if you've owned your business for decades, because learning is always beneficial. You won't get your rival across the street to give you advice, but industry leaders from across the country (and even the world) will give you fifteen minutes if you call them and ask for it.

Helping others taps into two innate needs successful business owners have:

1. The desire to help others: When owners achieve massive financial success, their goals tend to shift from making more money to helping others succeed.
2. The need to feed their ego: We all love to talk about ourselves, especially when we achieve something remarkable. Business owners are no different.

If those owners can offer validation for what you're doing, or point out pitfalls you need to avoid, the time and money you invest in that call or visit will be well spent.

AT THE END OF THE DAY, CARE ABOUT YOUR PEOPLE

We've talked a lot in this chapter about how business owners become strong leaders in their organization. I want to share one more story I hope illustrates a final point, and if you take away just one truth from this chapter, let it be this:

You must care about your people. If you don't, nothing else matters.

One of the salesman who worked for dad at the Hippodrome Ford dealership was Bob Suffridge, one of the most decorated football players who ever lived. He was a three-time All-American, won the Knute Rockne award for the nation's best lineman, made the College Football Hall of Fame, was named to the All-Time SEC Team, made the Hall of Fame for the Sugar, Rose, and Orange Bowls, and never lost a game during his career at the University of Tennessee. He was an All-Pro in the NFL with the Steelers and the Eagles, plus he served in the Navy during World War II as a lieutenant commander.

It seemed like everyone in Tennessee who wanted a new Ford bought it from Bob. Not only was he a celebrity, but he was also a wonderful human being. Everyone at Hippodrome loved Bob, and he fit beautifully into the tight-knit fabric of the dealership family.

Bob's life unraveled when he got a divorce and drank to cope. He was clearly depressed and got sloppier in his work the longer his drinking continued.

One Saturday morning, dad and I were walking across the service department floor, and Bob was coming at us. He had on a white dress shirt and a tie, the required attire. Underneath his shirt pocket was an inch-long tear through which you could see his undershirt.

What you must understand is, although my father was 6 feet, 5 inches tall, 250 pounds, and a former college athlete, he was a gentle giant. Sure, he was raised on a farm during the Great Depression and was tough as nails, but he never laid a hand on any of us four kids.

That said, I was shocked when, as we pulled even with Bob, dad put his finger in the tear and ripped Bob's shirt all the way to his waist. Bob and I were speechless. I mean, what the hell do you say when your dad rips anyone's shirt down to the waist, let alone a football Hall of Famer?

Dad looked at Bob and told him, "I want you to go to Joseph Frank's and pick out some new clothes. I'll call and tell them you're coming, and I'm going to pay for it."

Bob turned around, got in his car, and left.

I looked at dad and said, "I can't believe you did that."

"I've got to get his pride back," dad replied. "He can't do that looking like a bum."

When we got back to the office, dad called Joseph Frank, the fine men's clothing store where he bought his clothes, and told them to get Bob two suits, two sport coats, two pairs of dress slacks, a dozen dress shirts, a dozen ties, and two pairs of shoes.

A new wardrobe may not seem like a big deal, but when Bob came back to the dealership, you could tell from his walk and his smile his confidence was back.

He thanked dad, not for the clothes, but for the wake-up call.

Years later, I asked dad if he expensed the clothes he bought for Bob. His response taught me more about leadership than any book I could ever read.

"Absolutely not," he said. "Bob is my friend, and he needed help."

It's not enough to say you care about your employees. You should show it every day in ways big and small. You must genuinely care about them and possess a deep desire to see them succeed. Sometimes, that means giving them a wake-up call.

Other times, it means giving them specific feedback on a job well done.

Strong leadership leaves a lasting impression. Perhaps the biggest compliment I ever received was when a banker friend asked one of my managers from a company I had sold years before, "What's it like to work with Bob Bethel?"

The manager said, "If I heard Bob was going to move Monteagle Mountain (in southern Tennessee) in the morning, I'd show up with a shovel if that's all I had."

His answer wasn't as much about me as it was about all the things he had seen our team achieve that others said we couldn't do.

When you adopt the right behavior and have a heart for people, leadership will come easily, because people will want to follow you. From there, it's up to you to refine your leadership and continue looking for ways to better serve your team. Implementing the steps we've covered in this chapter can help you during this journey of improvement.

CONCLUSION

YOU NEVER HAVE TO FAIL

I lost my ego early in my career.

That's what happens when your business fails, the banks seize everything you own, you move your family into a rental house, and must survive on a shoestring budget.

Failure was one of the most painful experiences of my life, but it purged me of the notion that I was handsome, smart, rich, bulletproof, and radiation proof.

I hope you've learned from my mistakes and will take the steps necessary to save or safeguard your business from failure. No business is immune to failure, but the lessons in this book give you the best chance at long-term success.

In seventy-seven businesses over the course of fifty-two years, the approach we've outlined has never let me down.

I've made a lot of money in my career off the mistaken belief owners have that their business is somehow different from all the others. As we know, all businesses are alike, because they all depend on profit to survive. We're in the money-making business, plain and simple. If your organization is not profit-minded, your survival is dependent on money you can borrow from banks, take from investors, or pull from your own pockets.

What do these cash sources have in common? Eventually they all dry up.

Your business is not different, because you make a quality product, provide great service, take care of customers, or treat your employees well. Every owner would prescribe these attributes to their business. These traits should be expected, not bragged about.

To set yourself apart as different or special is to set yourself up for failure. Every business is going to face challenges, which means every owner must be prepared to respond. If your mind isn't focused on profit, you won't be able to recognize problems when they arise or have the tools to handle them. Before you know it, that Ferrari's gone off the cliff.

When that happens, all parties involved with the business—customers, employees, vendors, contractors, investors—will suffer right along with the owner.

The destiny of your business is in your hands.

When I think of that truth, I'm reminded of the story of two young boys who went up the mountain to see a wise man who was blind. One of them said, "Old man, in my hand is a bird. Is it dead or alive?" Knowing the boy's heart, the wise man answered, "My son, it is as you wish it."

Admitting you're in business to make money is making the choice to thrive and not just survive. Remember: It is not selfish to want to make money, but it is essential.

BUSINESS IS A BATTLEFIELD

As I've mentioned a couple times in this book, I have great admiration and respect for T. Boone Pickens, and what he's accomplished in his career. Here's a man who started with nothing and became adept at building teams that were profit-making machines driven by a plan.

Pickens is one of the many noted leaders who would say business is a battle, and this quote from his book, *The First Billion Is the Hardest*, illustrates his belief:

"Pressure is the great equalizer when it comes to talent and work ethic. Everyone takes punches in life. The difference between success and failure is not only getting back up after a punch, but then start punching back. As someone who's [sic] road to success has been very public, I can speak from experience. Get up quickly…then start swinging. It's the only way you can survive."

We are all fighting in the same marketplace to sell and make a profit. Even two businesses in different industries are competing against each other, because consumers only have so many dollars to spend. Whether they choose to buy a new mattress or remodel their back patio, for instance, largely comes down to how hard you fight to reach them.

If you study the men and women who've fought for decades to reach the top of their respective industries, you won't find buzzwords or complex theories, but you will find a lot of common sense. True leaders are interested in results, not flash and sizzle.

Successful business owners also love what they do.

Look at T. Boone Pickens, who's eighty-eight years old, or Warren Buffett, who's eighty-six. Neither of those men has needed to work for decades, yet they continue to hammer away well into their ninth decade on this planet, because they love their work and are still fulfilled by it.

I've been at this for five decades, but I still look forward to work every morning when I wake up, even though my job requires I continuously fight against failure.

Loving what you do gives you a reason to keep doing it, even when the chips are down, and the outlook is bleak. Toughness is born from a persistent, never-say-die attitude, and on the battlefield of business, toughness is an absolute necessity.

I believe the high failure rate within the first five years for new businesses is due in large part to owners whose intentions were misguided. Anyone who thinks starting or buying a business is their ticket to less work, more pay, and fewer problems is sadly mistaken. Owners with that mindset get punched and don't get back up.

You need a fighter's mentality if you're going to survive. One of the reasons I failed in my first business was I didn't want to fight. I wanted business ownership to be kind and gentle, but the world doesn't work that way. Now, I understand the first step after getting knocked down is to get up and hit back twice as hard.

At the same time, your fighter's mentality must be tempered with humility. Anyone who enters business ownership with pride in their heart will be humbled by their business at some point. I never go into a turnaround thinking I have the answers in hand. My secret to success is I'm smarter than everyone at knowing how dumb I am.

I never go into a new business and tell everyone what to do. As an outsider who's often stepping into a new industry, that would be an idiotic approach to take. Instead, I spend time talking with the employees and other industry leaders, soaking up all the knowledge I can about how my new business operates.

If you've owned your business for fifteen minutes or fifteen years, don't shut yourself off to learning. Allow that intellectual capital to flow into your business, so it can help you prosper. As Albert Einstein famously said, "Once you stop learning, you start dying."

Having been inside seventy-seven dying businesses, I can testify to the truth of Einstein's words.

FINAL WORDS OF ENCOURAGEMENT

When my oldest daughter was in high school, she was assigned a report explaining what her father did for a living. When she asked me to explain my job, I gave this answer:

"I use words to sell hope."

She got angry with me and stormed out of the room, because she thought my response was snide. I went and found her to explain what I meant by my answer. On paper, I told her, my job is to help turn around failing businesses for the banks. My concerns when I'm at work involve profitability, payroll, personnel, and pleasing the banks.

On a deeper level, my job is to bring out the best in everyone I work with, so we can use our God-given talents to collectively benefit the business. In businesses teetering near the edge, the turnaround begins with instilling hope in the minds of every employee. We all must believe the business can be saved before we can do it.

I accomplish this not through rah-rah speeches or fake hype, but by implementing the strategies we've covered in this book. I don't need to channel my inner salesmanship, when I can show the team our destination and explain the path we'll take to get there.

When the employees buy in to my hope, there's no limit to what we can accomplish.

If business struggles have knocked you flat on your back, it could be you need to inject some hope back into your business. The pages of this book are filled with hope, but that hope can only be effective if implemented. It's up to you to light that fire within your business. Change won't be easy, nor will fighting against the forces conspiring to bring your business down. Just remember, nothing worthwhile ever comes easy.

If owning a business was easy, everyone would be as rich as Bill Gates.

Just because it's difficult, doesn't mean you must fail.

The strategies in this book will prepare you for the rough times, so when you get knocked down, you can get up, and like T. Boone Pickens said, come out swinging.

ACKNOWLEDGMENTS

I'd like to thank my business partner, friend, and wife, Reese, who encouraged me to write this book and helped me every step of the way. Thanks to my children—Jackie, Robbie, Tommy, and Brittany—who have put up with my travel and long hours. A huge thanks to my son Tommy, who has been C.O.O. of our companies for the past seven years, allowing me time to help other companies implement the items outlined in this book.

I'm thankful for my business partner of twenty-five years, Chuck Ritzen, who was flying a relief mission to Haiti in 2016 when his plane crashed. I will miss him always.

To my Outliner, Nikki Van Noy, my Editor, Josh Raymer, and Kathleen Pedersen, my Publisher, without whom this book would never have happened.

ABOUT THE AUTHOR

BOB BETHEL is the orchestrator of seventy-seven business turnarounds over the past fifty years. His early successes and troubles in his career inspired Bob's passion for taking over struggling businesses and making them profitable. Bob has turned around companies in every industry imaginable and has helped save over ten thousand jobs. A graduate of the Owen Graduate School of Management at Vanderbilt University, Bob owns several businesses across the southern United States, is an Eagle Scout, and teaches three-day on-site seminars for all types of businesses.

For more details about booking private workshops, speaking engagements or training, visit www.robert thomasbethel.com or contact me at robertthomasbethel@ gmail.com.

65780286R00116

Made in the USA
Lexington, KY
24 July 2017